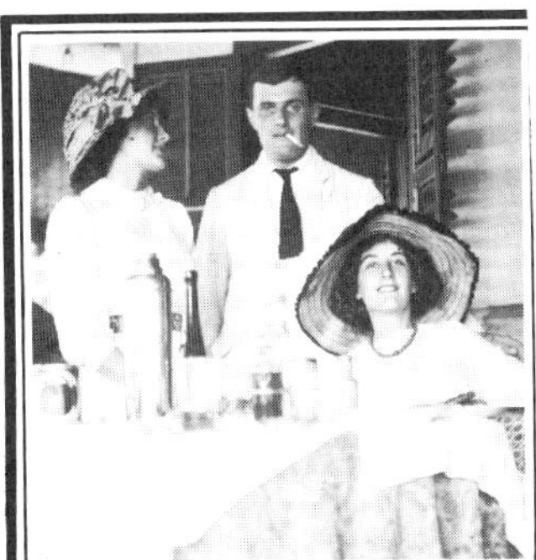

Photography

Richard Greenhill

Margaret Murray

Jo Spence

An *ideals* Publication
First Printing

ISBN 0-89542-900-4 295

Consultant
John H. White
Photojournalist
Chicago *Sun-Times*

Library of Congress Catalog Number: 80-80260

Printed and bound in U.S.A.

Published by Ideals Publishing Corporation
11315 Watertown Plank Road
Milwaukee, WI 53226

First published
Macdonald Educational Ltd.
Holywell House, Worship Street,
London EC2A 2EN

Contents

Why photography?

Much mystique surrounds the techniques and professional practices of photography, but in reality the basic craftsmanship involved is quite easy to learn. What many people find difficult is knowing what they want to say and discovering a means of saying it through pictures.

People have a variety of motives for becoming photographers, ranging from shyness to a need for self-expression. Photographs themselves can be taken for many different reasons: to communicate ideas, to understand ourselves better, to reveal hidden aspects of nature, as a social and educational tool, to record things as evidence, to entertain or decorate, to sell things, to make money, as an excuse for watching other people, to gain access to forbidden territory, to give us power — the list is endless. Anyone contemplating taking up a camera should ask themselves two main questions: what is the reason for using photography (as opposed to writing, for example), and for what purpose will the pictures be used?

Pictorialism and realism

As a method of communication, photography initially had a close affinity with painting, which led to a very personal branch of photography called *pictorialism*. This is concerned with aesthetic effects and the beauty of the single image. Later, with improved technology, new branches of photography developed. One of these was scientific photography and another was documentary photography, which attempted to record the "real world." When we try to reflect reality in this way we call it realism; but can we ever believe that it is truthful or realistic, or does it merely convey to us the ideas and beliefs of the photographer and his or her own particular society? Photography offers us other people's experiences, secondhand. There is an old saying that the camera never lies, whereas in fact it usually offers us only part of the truth, which can come very close to a lie. In pictorialism the question of truthfulness does not arise, for here the main concern is with the quality of the photographic image and in displaying the artistry of the photographer.

Who is photography for?

Most photography is a one-way process, especially if you choose to earn a living from it. Many professional photographers' lives consist of pleasing other people, performing on demand, in many cases with very little control over what they want to do. It is what the clients want done that matters.

Amateur photographers and semiprofessionals have much greater freedom in choosing who they work for and how they work. If you want to go beyond the family album and camera club competitions, you can get involved in some form of photography for your community or neighborhood. This could be a valuable asset in recording living conditions or as evidence in a planning dispute.

Pictures can be rephotographed and turned into slide shows that can be a basis for discussion. They can also be used as an ideal starting point for storytelling and learning to read. Visual aids have an immediacy and relevance both for adults and children which

▶ *Photography can reveal the hidden aspects of nature. A chicken embryo.*

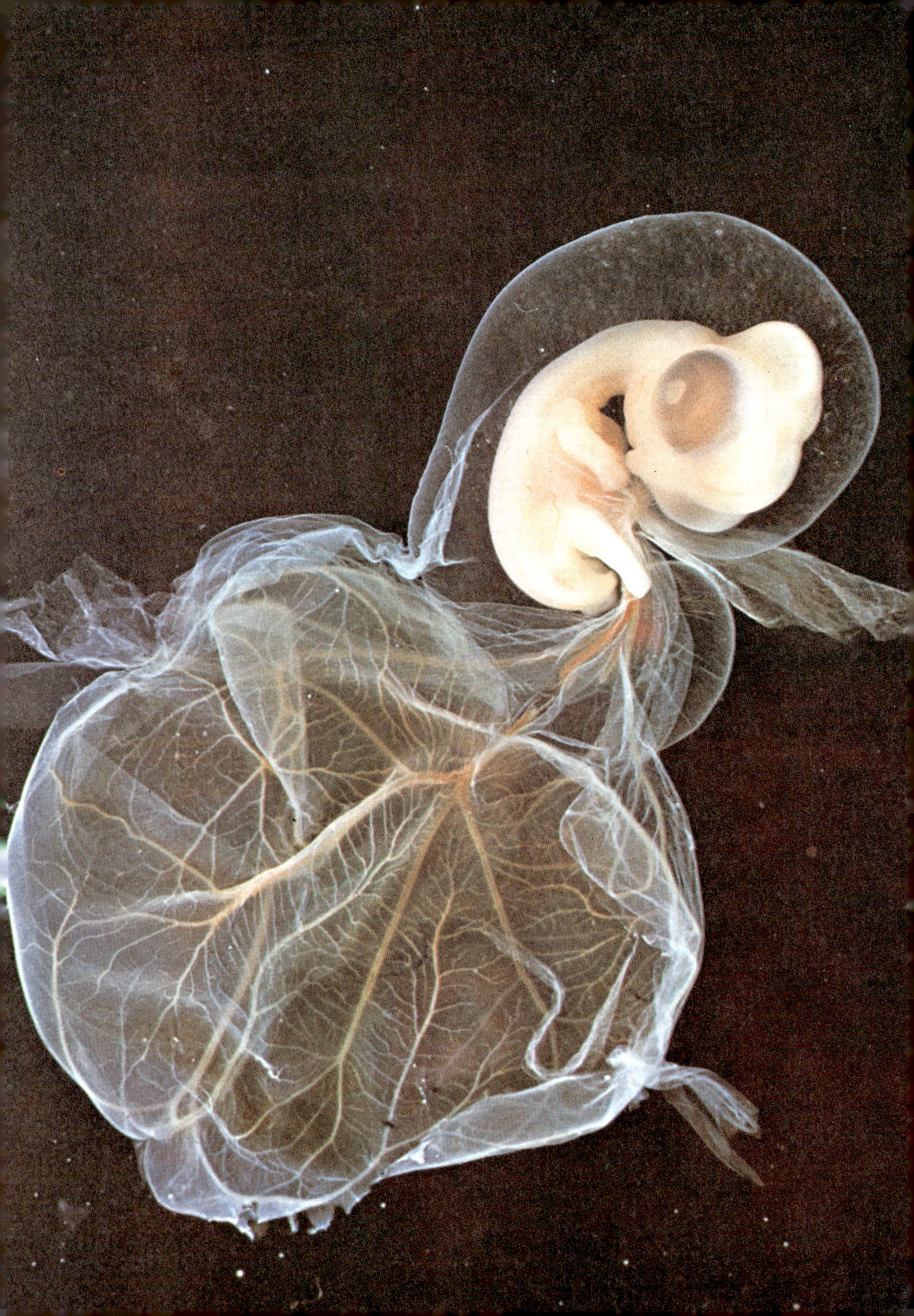

prepackaged books do not have. Family albums could even become part of local history projects; records of local events and architecture taken by you could in time become part of historical archives. All photographs are a form of history and as such are worth preserving for others to see.

In many ways, photography is inadequate for conveying abstract ideas or concepts. What it can do well is to represent surface information. It will, for example, show you exactly the house someone lives in, but it cannot explain why economic circumstances allow or force them to live in such a way.

Because of this limitation, some photographers work with sequences of pictures or photo essays and support their visual narrative with text or captions. Other photographers have found that even this does not go far enough for them to get their message across. They take several images, physically cut them up, and then reassemble them, thus creating a montage to which they can add a text if necessary. Experimentation along these lines can be exciting and productive.

Looking at photographs

We bring our own autobiographies with us when we look at or decode an image. We are always selecting or editing, consciously or unconsciously; we ignore bits we don't understand and give full rein to those we think we do.

There are many "realities": that of a single picture, of two pictures side by side, of a series of images, of images and text. Mass-reproduced images surround us: we see them in shops, books, magazines, on television and billboards, and in films. Many contain hidden

▼ *Family of pavement dwellers with all their possessions in Bombay, India.*

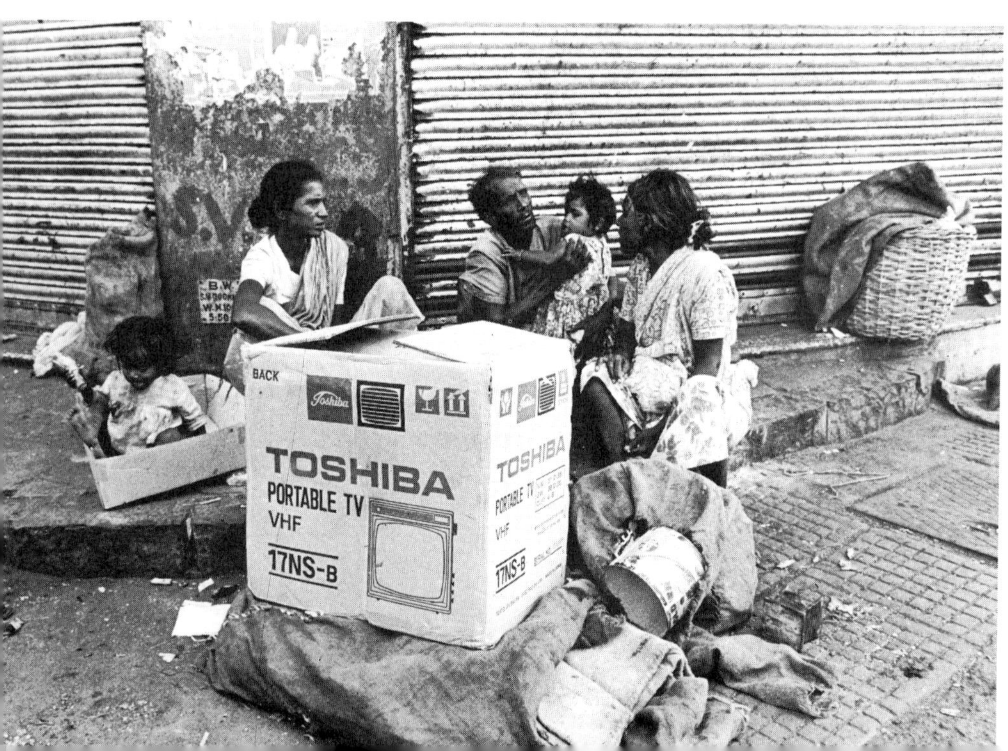

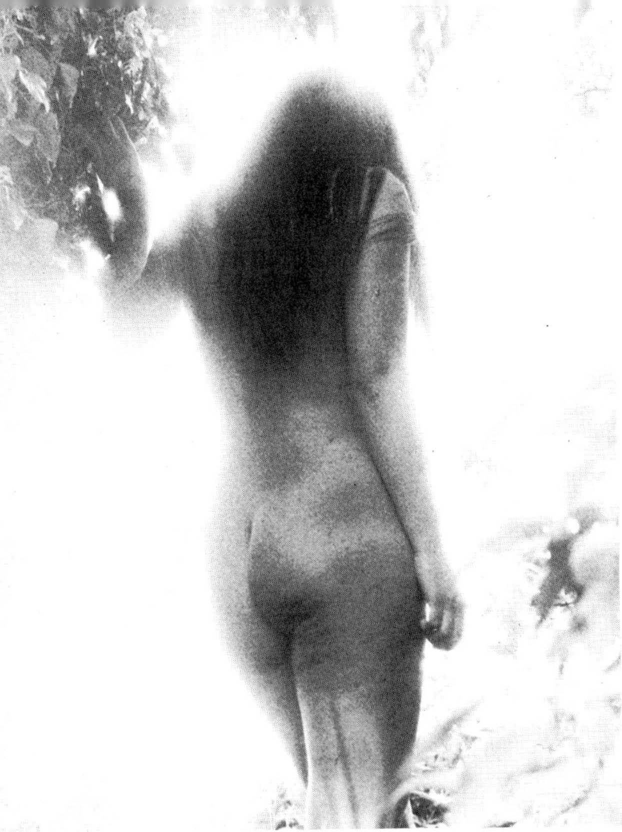

◀ *Pictorialism is concerned with aesthetic effects. It can degenerate into sentimentality or even "soft porn."*

messages that, when repeated over a period of time, can establish a new "reality" that helps to shape our ideas about what is normal or desirable. For example, we are led to believe that normal people must live in families of four, own an automatic washing machine, and drive a car. This visual reinforcement means that in time these messages can become part of our own experience, which is stored in our memories. When we choose to make our own images, do we just echo the dominant stereotypes and images of the mass media, or can we try to put forward our own version of reality, to show our own experience more accurately?

Pictures viewed years after an event will be analyzed differently from when they were taken. Pictures viewed out of context mean different things to different people, and the same picture can evoke quite different responses from various people, even if they like it. Think of a baby picture. To a woman it might mean love, to a man financial responsibility, to a baby food manufacturer profit, to a nurse work.

To shoot or not to shoot?

Images also influence the way others feel about people. Think of all the pictures we decide not to take when it comes to our family and friends. There are many aspects of our own lives which we are not prepared to reveal to others, such as pictures of us looking tired, stupid, or old. We hardly ever include in our albums pictures of ourselves at

Snaps

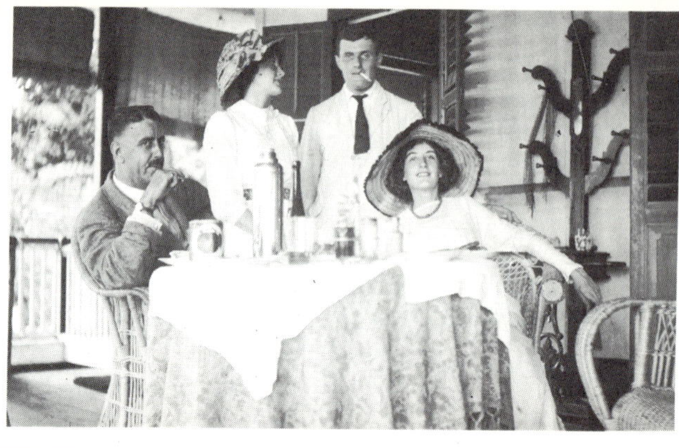

Snapshots showing three generations of one family.

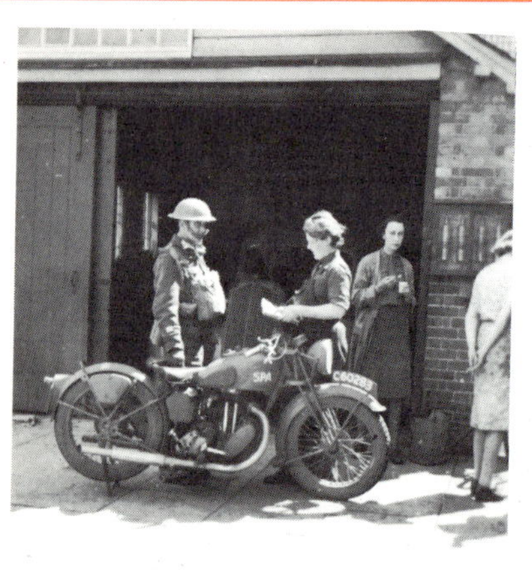

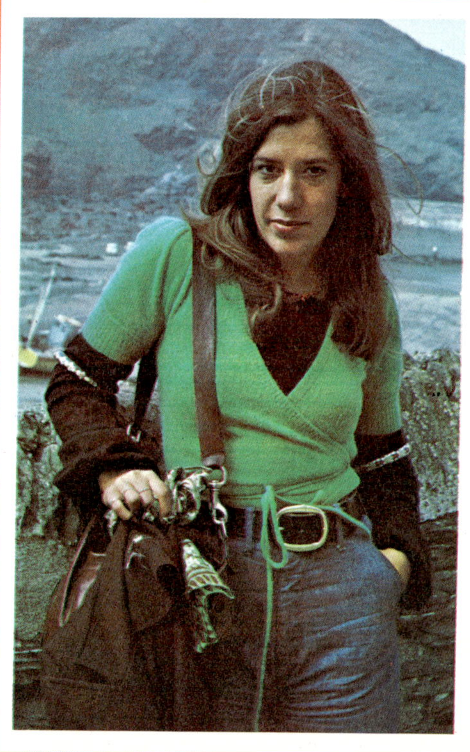

A page from a modern family album.

Only recently have people begun to realize the value of snapshots and family albums as a valuable source of personal and historical information. Sometimes the only evidence that whole families ever existed lies in the pages of their family albums, representing photography in its most innocent and least contrived form. Lifestyles and standards of living may have changed since the days when Kodak started a major craze in the 1890s with their slogan "You press the button, we do the rest," but the content of snapshots remains similar. Only the addition of color has added a new dimension.

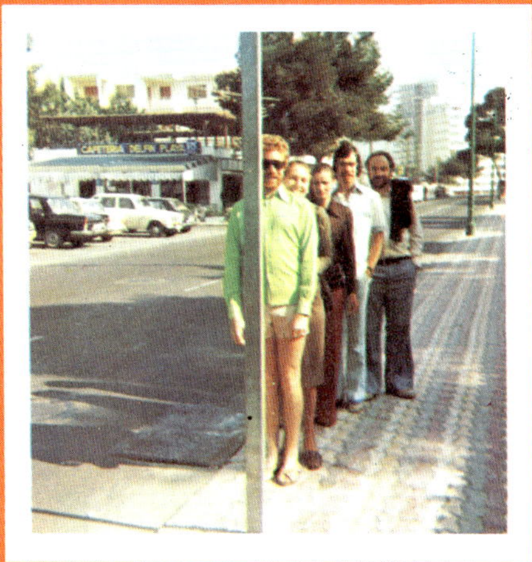

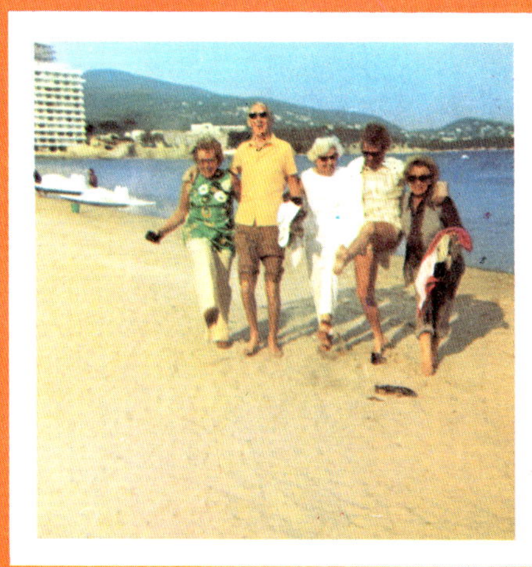

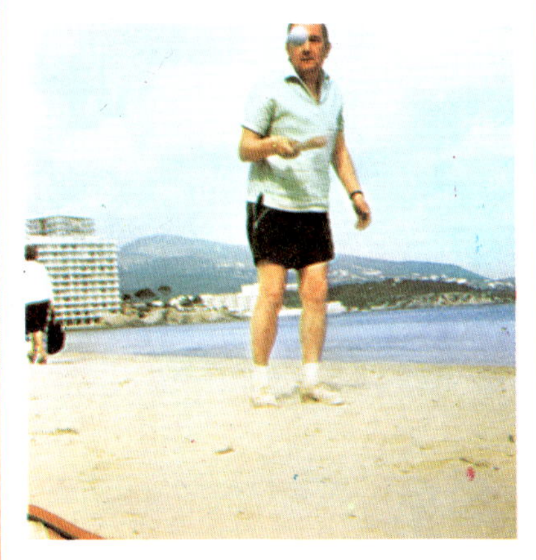

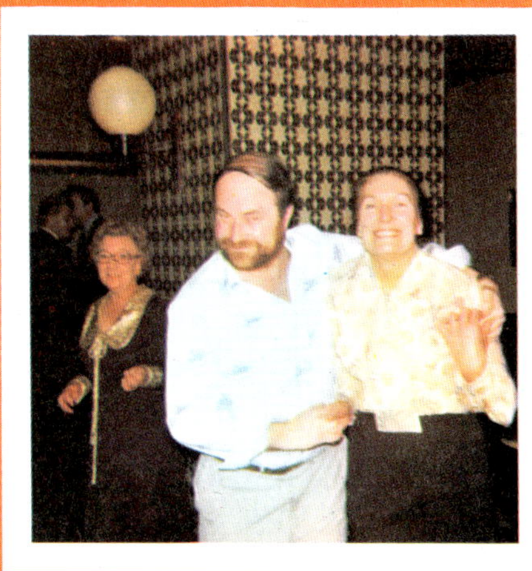

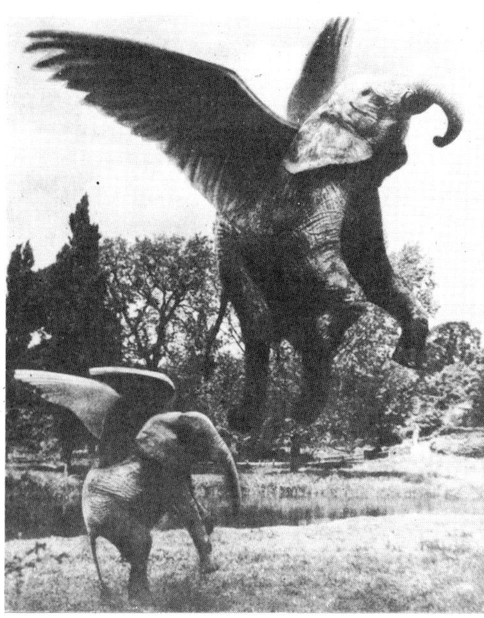

◀ *Some photographers found that a single or unmanipulated image just couldn't go far enough to convey ideas; they took several images, physically cut them up and then reassembled them. John Heartfield used this to devastating effect in his work. This picture was used on the front cover of the English news magazine* Picture Post *the week following Chamberlain's Munich agreement in 1938.*

work, wearing torn clothes, or with teeth missing. We aim to preserve and present an image of ourselves. Why do we so rarely photograph our family and friends as we photograph others?

Very often, in order to take pictures, we invade the privacy of people we don't know and will never meet again. In some countries this is against the law. But even if the subject's consent is obtained we then impose our own point of view, our own set of values onto what we see and record. Text and captions can also introduce misunderstandings. This is a major controversy in photography: to shoot or not to shoot? When we photograph people, would it be better if we returned to them with the results, discussed them, and asked for their opinions? How can we know if we misrepresent others? When taking pictures, it is vital to take all these questions into consideration.

This book is primarily an introduction to photography as a means of recording and representing the world. It concentrates on explaining simple skills and technology, encouraging the development of ideas but also on breaking down the mystique which still surrounds photography. At a time when the industry is increasingly dominated by a few large firms and costs are soaring, moves are beginning to be made away from photography for individuals by individuals toward the sharing of resources, skills, and results. Photography is a major form of communication that deserves to have time spent on understanding both its language and its limitations.

▶ *You certainly don't need to be old to take exciting pictures. In the early 1900s, when he was eight years old, Lartique took remarkable pictures of his eccentric and inventive family and friends. His perception of events was probably very different from that of the adults he so often depicted in his pictures. His early lack of inhibition was lost in his later pictures.*

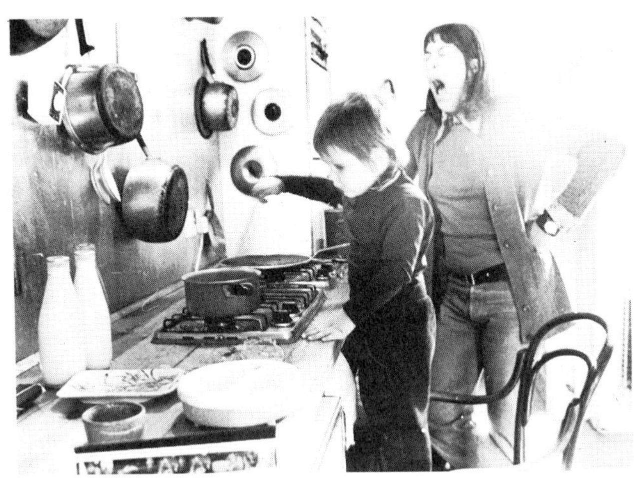

◀ *Very seldom do professional photographers turn the camera on their own families in the same way as they do to strangers. Here is one picture from a series by Richard Greenbill recording his own family.*

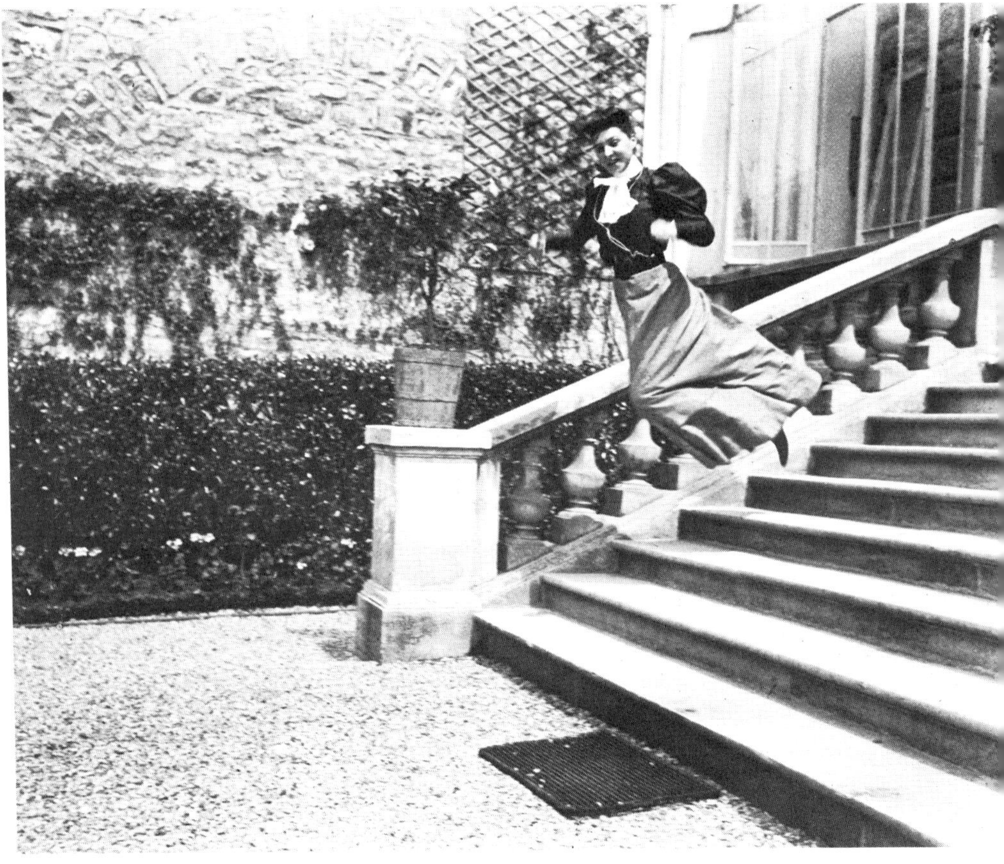

Bread and butter

Although considered the Cinderellas of photography, studio portrait photographers do a very useful job for many of us. They also form a bridge between the advanced amateur and the mysterious world of the professionals, often being the only contact that the general public has with those who earn their living by photography.

The job calls for an extraordinary mixture of capabilities. Half the time is spent coaxing the best expressions from tense sitters, or composing unwieldy wedding groups — the other half being locked away in the darkroom, developing and printing the results. On top of that, a good business brain is essential. Work varies a great deal and can range from attending a christening to recording an accident for a legal case. Experience is the only real teacher; success is very much a matter of trial and error.

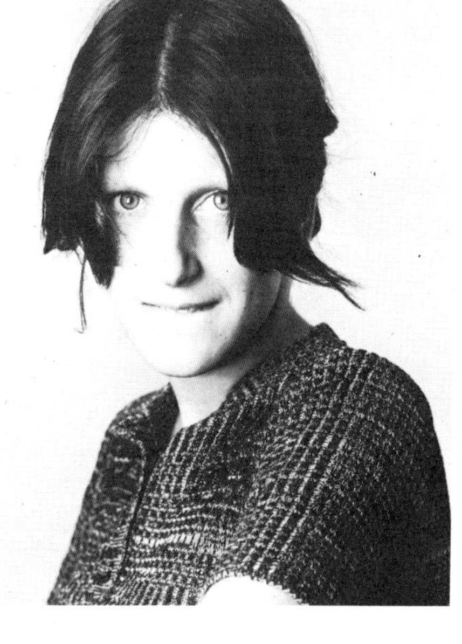

Portraiture

Of all the innumerable pictures taken since the inception of photography, the majority have been of people. So it follows that a major part of the work is portraiture. Essentially a good studio portrait is one that pleases the sitter. This is often achieved with a mixture of observation, cunning, and good technique. Contrary to what most manuals say about the subject, the best portraits are often sparingly lit.

Most books about portraits are illustrated with perfect faces. The reality of the studio is different. Over a period of time, all photographers develop their own series of set routines for dealing with the problems (real or imaginary) of double chins, bad skin, tired-

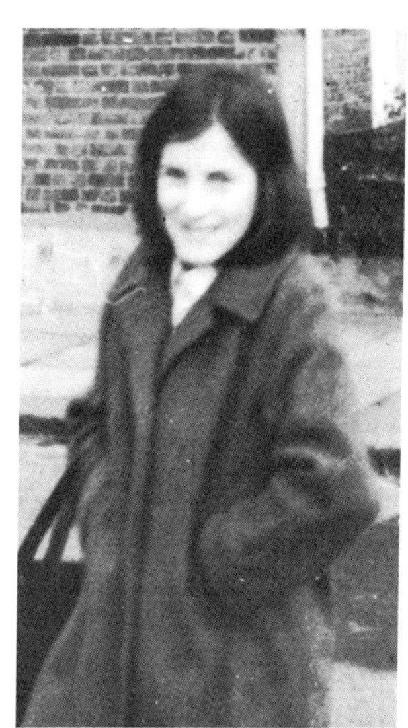

ness, big ears, buck teeth, protruding eyes, etc., not to mention subjects who arrive flushed and breathless from dropping their children off at school on their way. Implicit in taking a portrait is the notion that subjects want to present their best possible face for posterity, and in no way is there encouragement for photographers to take "realistic" portraits, for this would be contrary to expectations.

Fashions are continually changing in photography, with annual competitions (with big prizes) now being held for the most pleasant-looking child. This undoubtedly helps to establish new models of appearance for us all to aspire to both in our own lives and with our cameras. Emphasis is slowly moving toward more and more use of color film.

Weddings

The other mainstay of local studios is wedding photography. To watch an experienced wedding photographer is to see a time-honored ritual, as series of tableaux are enacted and recorded outside countless churches and justice of the peace offices every weekend. Photographing a wedding requires firm control, but never bossiness, on the part of the photographer. This is a difficult balance to achieve and adds to the nervous strain of knowing that there will be no chance to reshoot if disaster occurs. Wedding albums and photographs are valued by people long after events and memories have faded — sometimes even after the couple has parted!

◀ *Most books about portraiture are illustrated with perfect faces. The reality of the studio is different. Here we see a portrait by a professional photographer and a snapshot of the same girl.*

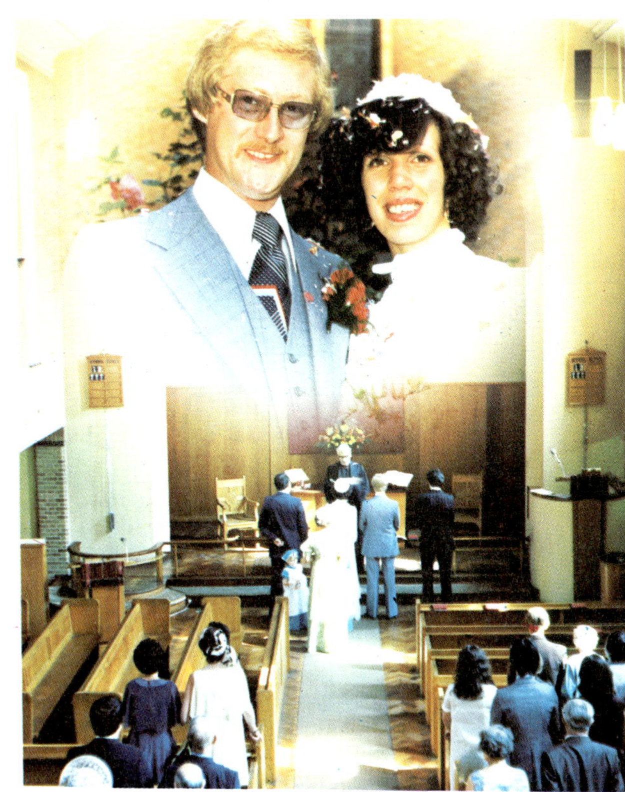

▶ *A typical modern wedding photograph taken by a studio photographer. The effect is produced by double printing.*

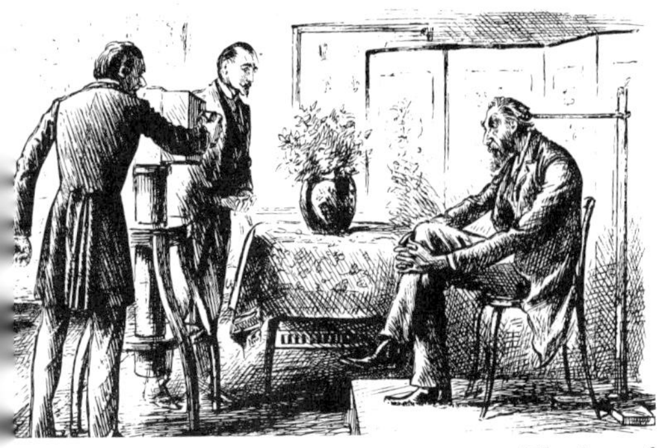

▲ Punch *cartoon, August 28, 1886: The Joys of Photography. Photographer (about to make his fourteenth attempt). "Could you manage to look a little less dreary, Sir — just for a half a second — not more!"*

People all adopt special faces and stances for the camera. Children put on acts learned from television — the advent of Kung Fu nearly drove photographers crazy for a while! Adults, ever mindful of their self-image, tend to sink rapidly into rigid terror, or else position themselves so that their "best face" is always showing to the camera, regardless of how many times they are moved by the photographer. A lot of tact and patience is needed to deal with these situations and to help people to relax and reveal themselves.

Many studios now use electronic flash for lighting portraits and groups of people. This is a welcome advance on the cumbersome and hot lighting of the past, and can be used in both black and white and color work. The flash goes off for 1/1000th of a second, which helps to prevent blurry pictures if sitters fidget or continually change expressions. This can be linked to a motorized-drive 35mm camera that allows shots to be taken in rapid succession. The ease with which such equipment can be used often encourages photographers to overshoot in the vain hope that something good will come of a session. This is a far cry from the days when a sitter had to remain motionless for up to five minutes because of the limitations of materials and equipment.

Most studio photographers are one-man bands, doing many different jobs from dawn to sunset. Between booking appointments, shooting, developing, printing, mounting, public relations, accounting, and collecting the cash, there is hardly any time to grab a meal or to have any sort of family or social life. There is great satisfaction, though, in working directly with people, in carrying out their wishes and in knowing that they are pleased and will recommend you to others. This is one of the few branches of photography in which the photographer can be involved in all stages of the work, from clicking the shutter to delivering the final prints. On the ability to cope with all this rests success or failure.

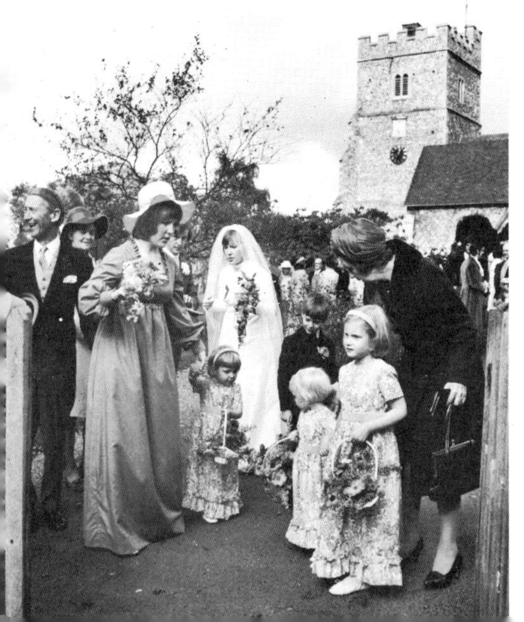

◀ *A typical wedding group before the photographer imposed some order on the scene.*

Social documentary

Various categories of photographers set out to record our relationships with the world and each other. Some documentary photographers do it in depth and often with sensitivity. Others have less time, such as press photographers who are more interested in news and less in everyday life and circumstances. Traditionally, photojournalism and documentary photography have been carried out by people with a genuine involvement or interest in their subject. Chris Bonnington is known as a photographer of mountaineering to photographers, but as a mountaineer who takes pictures to mountaineers.

Photographers who record social problems are often, but not always, concerned about the difficulties they illustrate. Because of the nature of the events and relationships recorded by these photographers, social documentation is one of the areas most beset with questions of ethics and responsibility. It is here that the basic question is raised "What

▼ *Five year old boy selling newspapers, photographed in 1905 by the sociologist Hine, who campaigned to get illegal child labor stopped in the United States.*

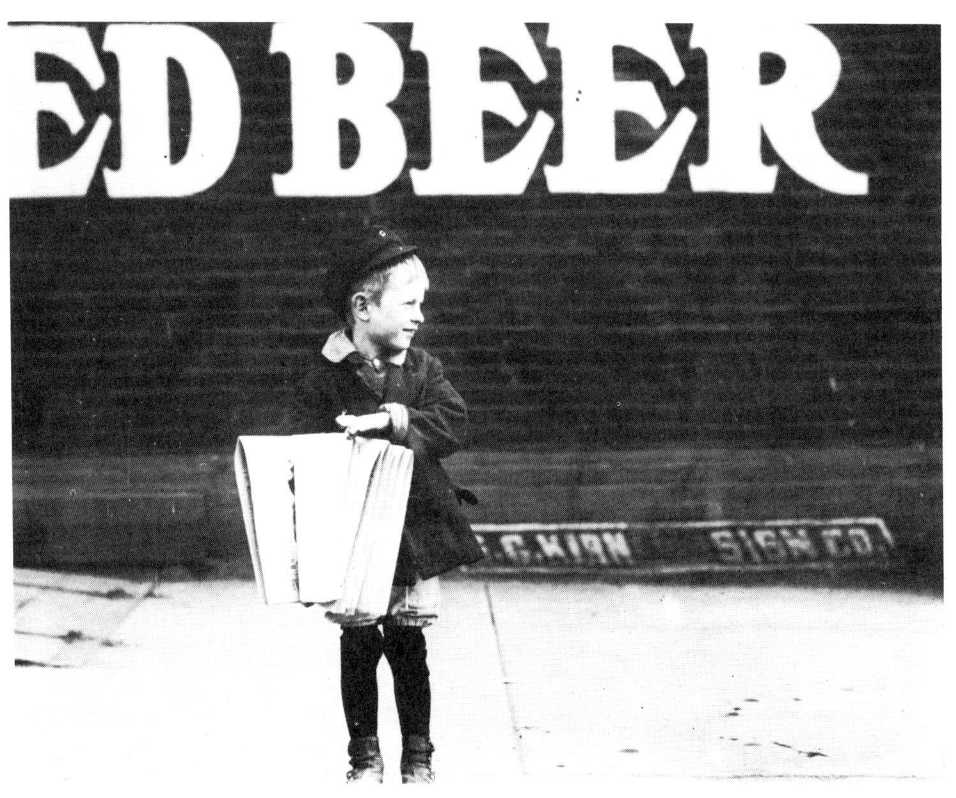

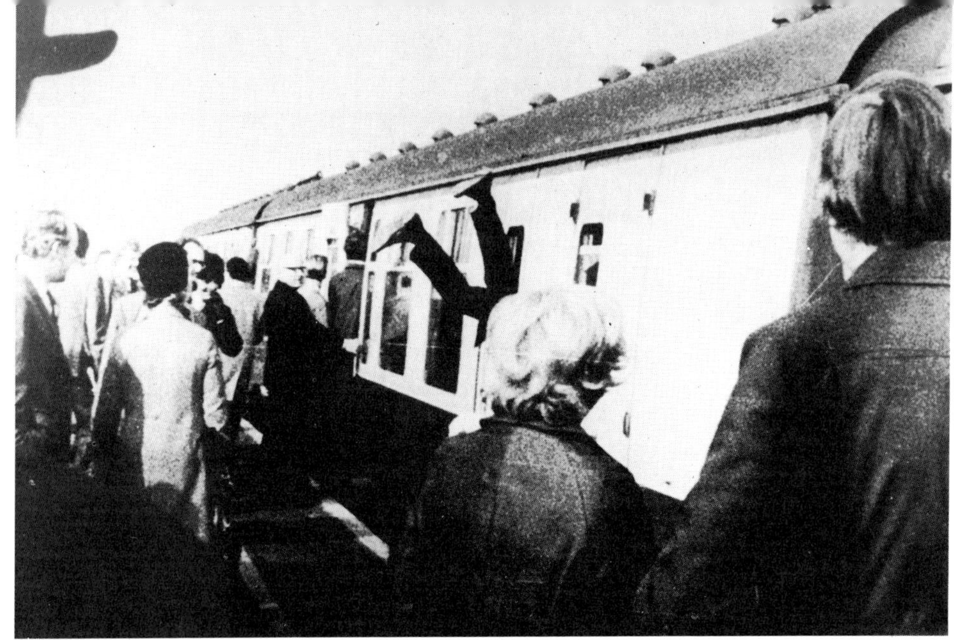

▲ *Some "snatched" pictures do not raise ethical problems. The essence of this photograph is its content — its poor technical content hardly matters.*

right have we to take pictures of people without their permission?" In certain countries it actually is illegal. Many photographs of social importance have been snatched without the subject's consent — as we rightly say, the photographs are "taken."

Sometimes this is not important, but at other times people become enraged and physically attack or sue photographers for what they consider a breach of privacy. The right to picture wars, famine, distress and misery is often questioned.

Although a careful analysis of a situation may have been done earlier, when they take pictures most photojournalists work intuitively. They are trying to record people "as they really are," being natural and sometimes under stress. In order to do this it is necessary to use light and inconspicuous equipment. This type of photography involves relatively low-level technology pushed to its limits. The photographer has to work fast, often in poor lighting conditions. This means trying to get the most in speed and sensitivity out of cameras, films, and lenses. Photographic quality often suffers, but in this area it is the content of a picture that matters more than its form. Photojournalists may wish or hope for beautiful lighting, but their main problem is often whether there is enough light to make an exposure at all.

In social documentation, the major means of subject manipulation is selection — and some things never get selected. The initial choice of subject matter, who or what is chosen to illustrate it, and the viewpoint the picture is taken from all come under this category. The photojournalist will rarely have any direct control over the subject in the way that a still life photographer has. A good example of this is travel photography.

For most of us, our view of other countries comes via photographs, motion pictures, and television. This view is often biased because photographers and filmmakers, amateur and professional, fail to recognize the reality of near-mythical places. They continue to record only well-known landscapes or images fitting preconceived ideas. In Paris it is always the Eiffel Tower, in India the beggars or the Taj Mahal, in Greece the Parthenon and the beaches. Often the vision records other countries as primitive and usually is many years out of date. The ox-plowing and hand-weaving are always pictured, but rarely are the parking meters, the modern factories, and the electric oven. We start to understand this when we see how wrong or one-sided information about our own country can be.

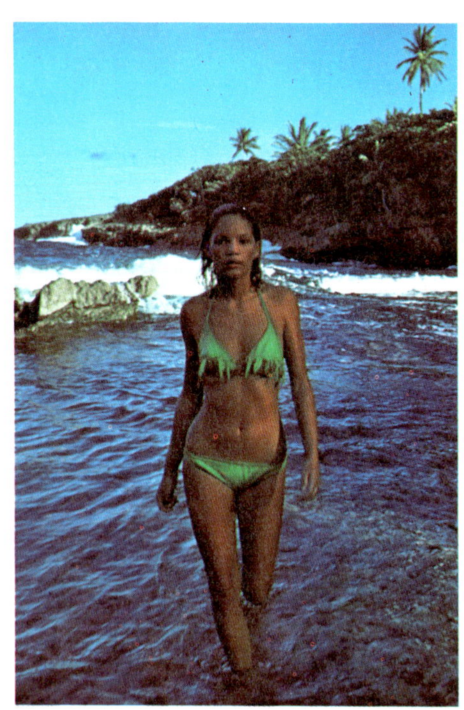

Travel photography is a good illustration of how photographs can give us a false picture of places and situations.

▸ *From a Jamaica Tourist Board advertisement.*

▾ *A middle-income housing development in Jamaica.*

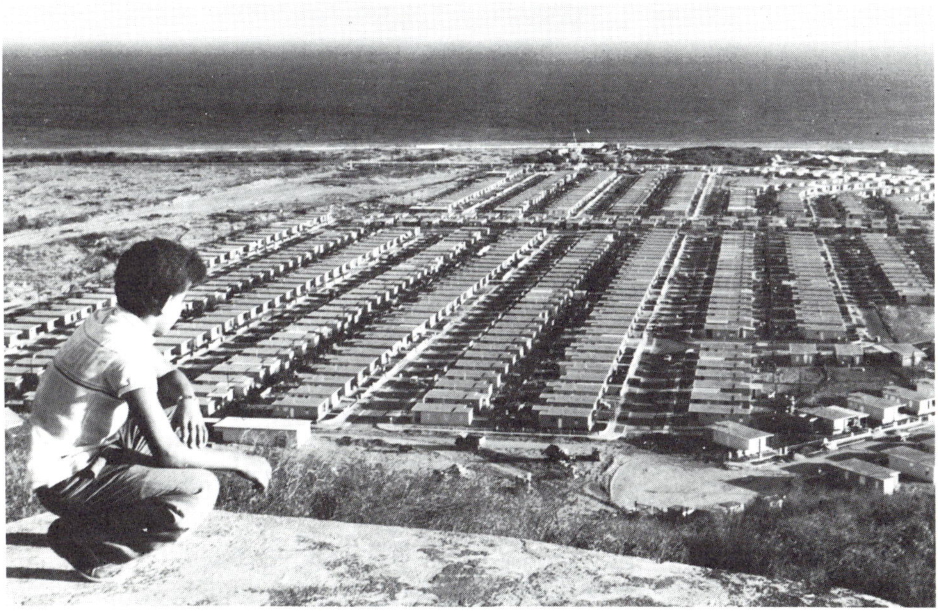

In order to take candid and unposed photographs, various techniques, work methods, and philosophies are employed. It is possible to use special telephoto lenses which enable close-ups to be taken from a distance. These are difficult to focus and hold still and produce an image in which the perspective is flat and rather unreal. They also raise ethical questions, since some can be used hundreds of yards away from the subject and are virtually "spy" lenses. In recent years there has been controversy surrounding press and magazine photographers who obtain pictures of famous people in this and other rather dubious ways. Obviously the technique has valid uses, but "telelenses" should be used with discretion.

Many good photographers learn to become inconspicuous, waiting until the moment is exactly right to take a picture. Henri Cartier-Bresson was one of the first photographers to talk about this method, which he developed into a philosophy he called "The Decisive Moment." Still other photographers introduce themselves into a situation, explain their presence, and wait until people are bored with them before starting to take pictures. This takes time and real involvement with the subject.

Press photographers are often criticized for the brash way they push into situations and insist on getting pictures, using flashbulbs and sometimes even literally putting their foot in the door. They work under strict deadlines, since most of us expect to see pictures of dramatic or interesting events we hear about almost instantly. It is this pressure that the press photographer is trying to satisfy. It is difficult to categorize photographers in this area, especially since many of the best fit into several pigeonholes or into none. Few of them are highly paid. Even the most respected in the world, such as Marc Riboud, are unlikely to earn as much as their equivalents in advertising or prestige industrial photography. The work is varied, often difficult, and sometimes dangerous. For better or for worse our own view of the world is influenced or formed by the pictures these photographers record for us.

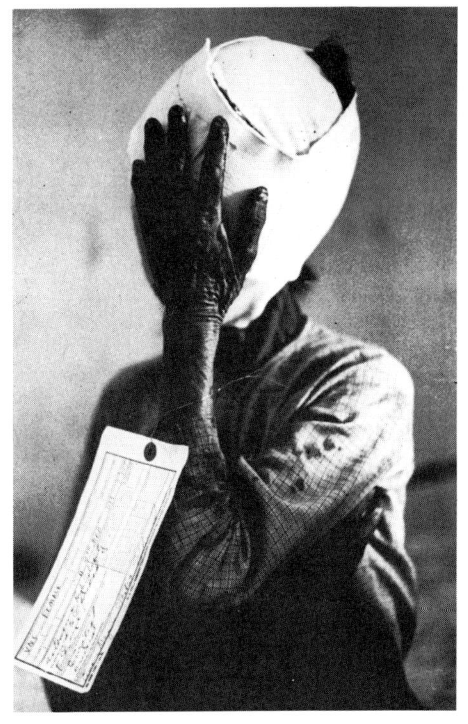

Throughout the history of photojournalism there have been people who have been aware that the power of credibility that photographs have means that they must be taken and used responsibly. One of the difficulties with this is that only very rarely does the photographer have any control at all over the way his or her pictures are used in a publication. It is nearly always the publication's picture editor who decides. He or she may frame the picture differently, put a misleading caption under it, or even juxtapose it so that its content is distorted. Of course, this does not invariably happen, but the fact remains that the photographer is not involved in the final use of his or her picture. Another problem is the media's obsession with the single picture. Very often a subject can be shown better through a series of pictures or a sequence. This can give greater depth, such as a historical or time dimension, a contrast which disturbs us, or further information which changes our original view.

Groups and individuals, both amateur and professional, have tried to overcome these difficulties by working on projects they initiate themselves and by finding new ways of publishing or showing their pictures. The projects have often included written material, since the majority of journalistic and documentary pictures are more valuable if additional facts are supplied with them. In the United States there often has been support for young documentary photographers. In the 1930s and 1940s the Photo League in New York gave instruction in all aspects of reportage, and students and teachers recorded the life in the streets of the city. The Concerned Photographers Group now produces educational programs and gives grants. Perhaps most famous of all, the Farm Security Administration, employed photographers — as well as journalists and artists — to show the life of the countryside during the Depression to urban Americans.

Photography can be a tool to explain people to people or it can send us inaccurate messages. It is not true that the camera does not lie. It does, but subtly. "There is a social responsibility implicit in the use of a language with so much power... its inherent quality of believableness is a challenge to the reader's sense of truth." (From *Photography is a Language*, by Whiting.)

◀ *A wounded woman. From Phillip Jones Griffiths' book* Vietnam Inc. *which he produced himself.*

▼ *Men watching a circus by Henri Cartier-Bresson the French photojournalist who has written about his philosophy of photography in* The Decisive Moment.

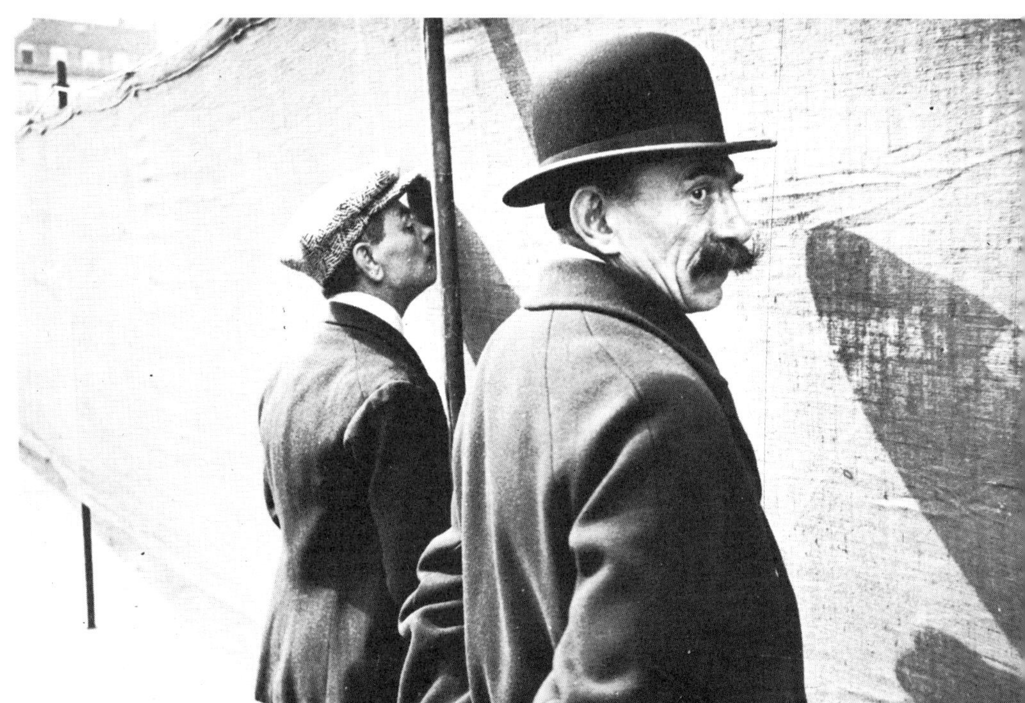

Advertising: constructing a dream

Advertising photography is characterized particularly by its working method. This is the analysis of the selling requirements of the picture, followed by the construction of the picture, using the highest standards of technique and creativity to have total control over the resulting image.

An advertisement is often conceived over a period of months by an advertising agency, which may reject fifty ideas for each one used. An art director chooses and briefs a photographer, and they agree upon a fee. A photographer can earn ten times more for a day's shooting for advertising than for a newspaper or magazine. The photographer uses a stylist to find props, a home economist to prepare food, a set builder, hairdresser, make-up artists, and so on to create the perfectly artificial world of the advertisement's picture. Film is used copiously and usually is charged to the client; 8 x 10 inch sheet film is widely used in advertising, as it gives a clear, sharp, realistic look to the picture, but it is expensive. Each picture is "bracketed," that is, exposures slightly darker and lighter than the correct one are made as well. (Blockmakers generally prefer a transparency to be a little on the dark side.) The large format size also facilitates retouching, which is often extensive. For example, a pack of cigarettes photographed in a setting often is replaced by a heavily retouched pack, shot in the studio, which is "stripped in" afterward.

Incredible care is taken in the preparation of the product and accessories. Labels are removed from bottles and flawless ones stuck on to replace them. These labels are then lit individually by small reflectors placed just outside the picture area. Behind each bottle or glass of beer or wine a tiny reflector is carefully angled to catch light and shine through the liquid towards the camera. Dew is sprayed onto flowers with a small gardening spray. Models' faces have reflectors aimed at them to lighten the shadows. The product itself is emphasized by being placed on a contrasting background. Wide-angle lenses are often used to enable more background material to be squeezed in, while keeping the product in the foreground as large as possible. The foam on a cup of cocoa is shaped and cajoled around and around till the correct shape occurs. Still life photographers, or their assistants, spend hours selecting perfect peas or even perfect grains of rice for arrangement on the top of a dish. No pains are spared in order to put together the final, totally controlled, image.

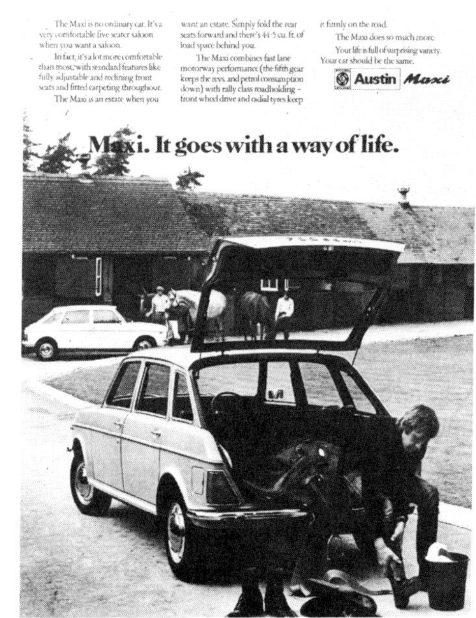

Hard and soft sell

The advertisement is a message on several different levels. On the conscious level, the message is simply an urge to buy. Advertisements where this predominates are known as *hard sell,* e.g., "Blanko Washes Whiter!" You can consider the assertion and even agree or disagree with it.

On a second level — and pictures stressing this are called *soft sell* — the message is received less consciously. An implication contained in the picture is, "If you buy this product you will be more successful, or happy." Symbols of wealth, success, or happiness are carefully chosen and included in the picture, with the knowledge that the viewer will unconsciously associate the product with them.

Sometimes the opposite implication is made, such as: "Without this product you will be unsuccessful or unhappy" or "Your children will lose out if you don't get...." In this case guilt becomes the means of persuasion.

On a third level, the picture will often contain elements of an even more indirect message. The advertiser tends to sell more products if the public follows a certain life-

▶ *Back projection or montage are often used to create advertising fantasy, but in this case the set was constructed and shipped to Istanbul, just for this picture.*

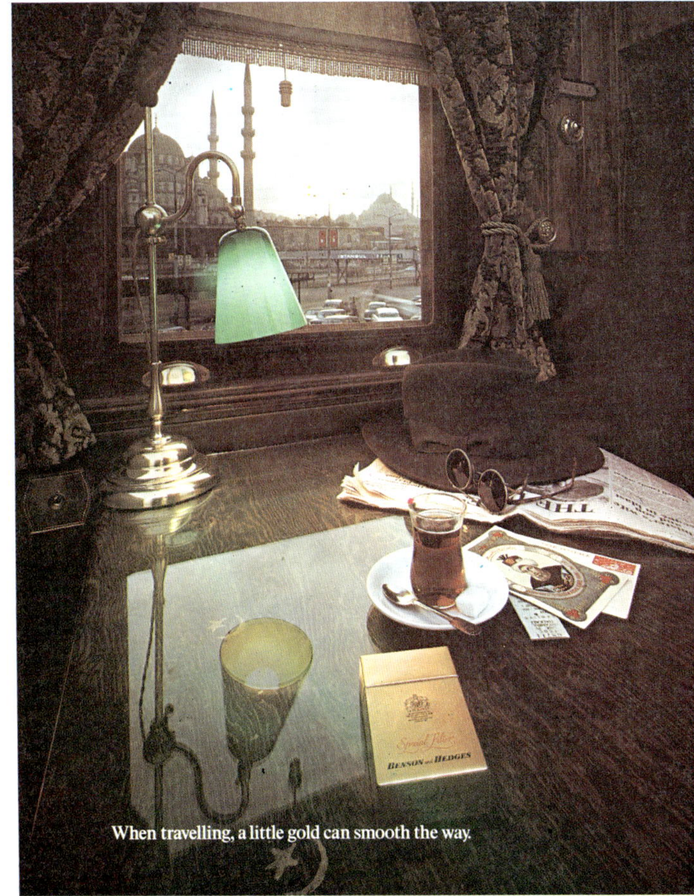

◀ *Advertisers know that the car is not just a means for getting from A to B. They sell it by selling an image for us to aspire to, a (better) way of life.*

style. Of course, the main effort of each advertisement is to increase sales of the product immediately, but if secondary messages can be included which reinforce a certain (high-spending) lifestyle, this is bound to help.

So, just as children copy models of a particular way of life in the behavior of their parents and other adults, in the characters in their books, and on television, in the same way the overall illusion — built up by the thousands of advertisements we see of an idealized lifestyle — becomes part of the overall experience of adults. Because the values taken for granted in all advertisements are exactly the same, we cannot help but absorb them. These values are implied, so we cannot agree or disagree with them, and they affect us without our knowledge. They suggest, silently, that all the wretched, silly problems we have can be eased away if only we will join the beautiful people who surround themselves with perfect taste, perfect stereo, perfect cigarettes, perfect gasoline, and so on. This illusion is helped by the popular belief in the truthfulness of the camera, which is the reason why photography dominates the advertising world.

▼ *Advertising on the conscious level. In this case the consumer is fully aware of the straightforward urge to buy for stated reasons. Apologists for advertising assert that this is its main function.*

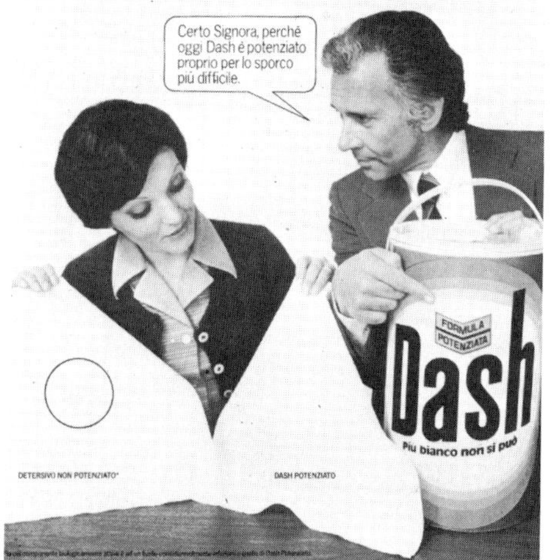

Fashion photography

In fashion photography there is no analysis and construction of the picture such as takes place in advertising. The photographer works more or less spontaneously, hoping that something valuable will develop during the session, which can be captured by the camera.

Although fashion is a branch of advertising, it cannot be totally controlled or analyzed. You either like it or you don't. Some magazines insist that the clothes be shown clearly, in some cases so clearly that readers can make them up themselves from the photographs. Others sacrifice detail in the clothes in favor of more freedom to create exciting images. Fashion models train to produce on request, gestures and expressions which have specific meanings. "Look sexy," "Look angry," "Look warm and approachable," "Look exciting."

As women gain more equality in our society, there has been a subtle but important change in the way models are shown in fashion pictures. They used to be portrayed entirely as "objects" — that is, there was no implication that they actually did anything as people, such as collect the kids from school, go to work, or just have a good conversation. They existed entirely as beautiful, sexy, or sophisticated objects of admiration. Now it is possible, even normal, to show women fashion models taking part in various activities; even if they are in the studio on a white background, the fact that they are often laughing (not smiling coyly), talking, frowning, or gesturing, implies some sort of participation as people in a living situation.

Men, on the other hand, usually have been photographed as subjects (people doing things). Male fashion models command, direct, point, step purposefully out of cars, always on their way to do something important. A good tip for a would-be fashion photographer might be to take some fashion pictures of men as objects — pose them so that their bodies make interesting shapes, light them beautifully, and blow their hair and clothes around with a wind machine or a large fan.

Fashion photography is one of the least difficult areas of photography to break into. You don't need nearly as much equipment, knowledge, or experience as with most other fields. All you need is genius!

All this applies to editorial fashion photography. Another branch, mail order and catalog fashion, is far more controlled at the preshooting stage. This is because the requirements of showing the clothes clearly and fitting a preconceived layout are often paramount. Spontaneity runs a poor third, so the photographer may have to work to a precise tracing that is placed over the viewing screen of the camera. These pictures are for people who will actually buy the clothes on the strength of the photograph, and who may return them if they do not think that they correspond to it, so that it is vital that every detail is shown clearly and correctly.

An example of the growing tendency to photograph women as people who lead lives of their own — even if these ways of life are available to only a select few.

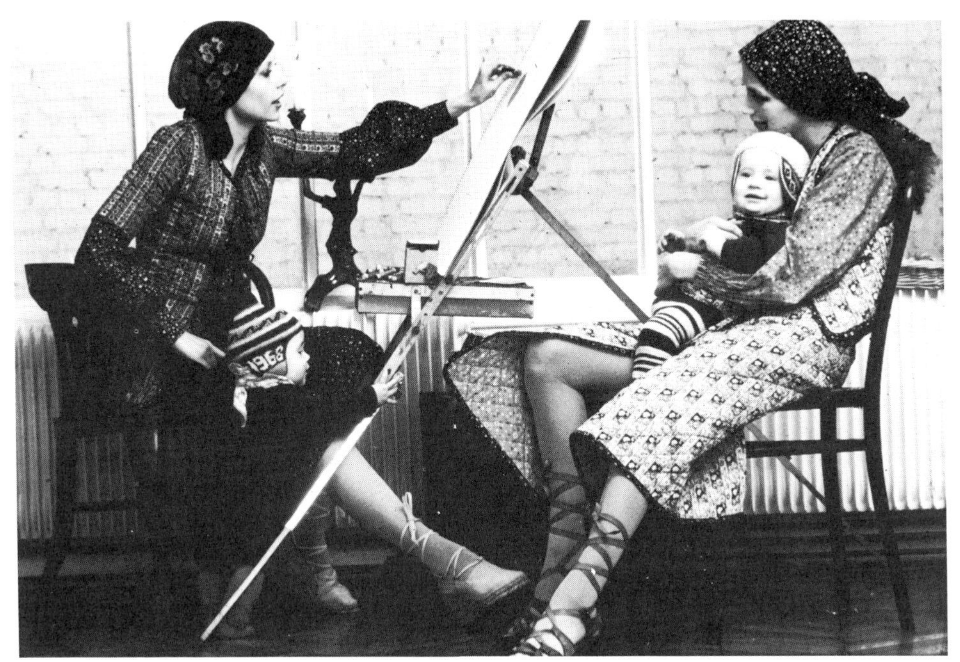

IMAGE FORMATION

Light travels in straight lines. When it strikes an object some of it is absorbed, some reflected. Shiny objects reflect light in a particular direction, but most objects are matt, so they scatter it. Reflected rays of light spread out in every direction. Lenses and other systems producing images work on the principle of collecting some of the rays diverging from one point on the subject and allowing them to fall on a particular point on a surface, while preventing rays reflected by other points from falling on that same surface point. This point is now an image of the point on the original subject, and will vary according to the brightness and color of the "subject point." If every point on the subject is reproduced in this way an image of the whole subject is built up.

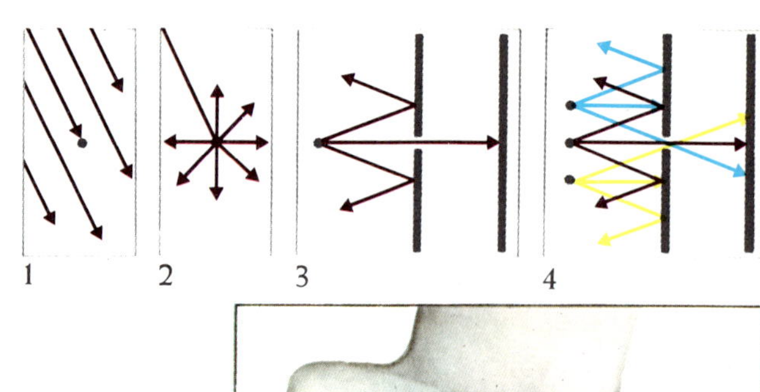

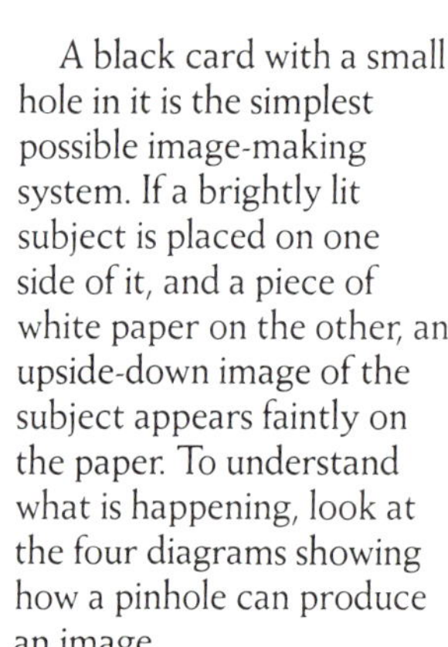

A black card with a small hole in it is the simplest possible image-making system. If a brightly lit subject is placed on one side of it, and a piece of white paper on the other, an upside-down image of the subject appears faintly on the paper. To understand what is happening, look at the four diagrams showing how a pinhole can produce an image.

In diagram **1** light strikes a point on the subject. In **2** this light is reflected in all directions. One single ray is able to pass through a pinhole in a piece of card. All the other rays are reflected or absorbed (diagram **3**). In diagram **4** two other subject-points are shown. From each of these only a single ray is able to pass through the pinhole. The "successful" ray from the upper subject-point strikes the surface below center, while that from the lower point can only strike it above center. The image is therefore upside-down. An image of each of the infinite number of subject-points which go to make up a face is produced in the same way, making an inverted image of the face.

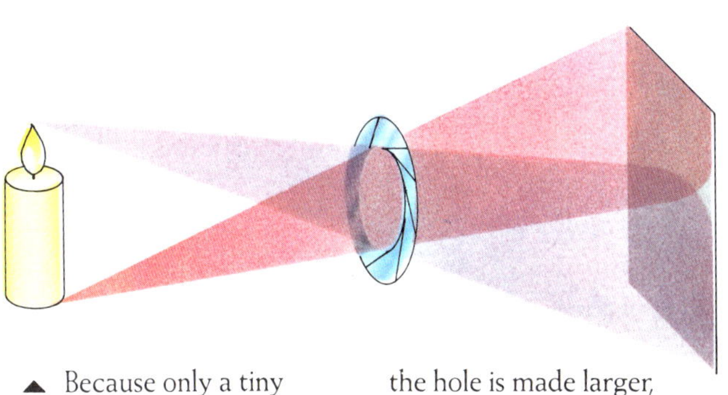

▲ Because only a tiny amount of light reflected by the subject can pass through the pinhole, the image is very weak, and a long exposure time is needed to record it on film. But if the hole is made larger, light from one subject point will spread out or diverge so as to overlap onto light from other subject-points. The result is a blurred image.

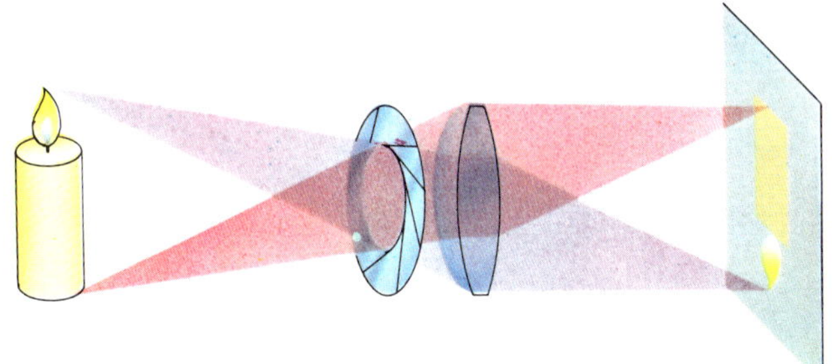

▲ To avoid this a convex lens is used; this causes rays of light to converge to a point; the diverging light rays are thus focused back into points, but are brighter than through a pinhole, as more of the light rays reflected by the subject have been collected.

The magic of film

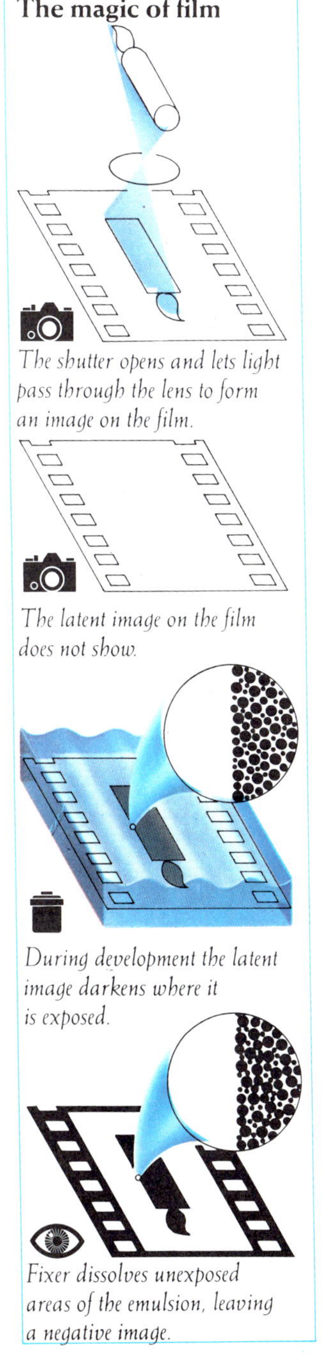

The shutter opens and lets light pass through the lens to form an image on the film.

The latent image on the film does not show.

During development the latent image darkens where it is exposed.

Fixer dissolves unexposed areas of the emulsion, leaving a negative image.

ALL CAMERAS ARE BASICALLY THE SAME

Although cameras cost from a few dollars to thousands of dollars, they all work on the same principles. They consist of a light-proof box with a system for holding film flat, a lens to form an image, and a mechanism for controlling the time the image falls onto the light-sensitive film. Even a homemade pinhole camera works like this.

1. Light-proof box. A shoe box — molded plastic or engineered metal.
2. Shutter mechanism. Piece of black masking tape or complex mechanical/electronic system to give range of accurate exposure times from 1 sec. to 1/1000 sec.
3. Lens and aperture. A pinhole serves both functions. The lens of a complex camera gives a brighter, sharper image and the aperture can be varied to control the amount of light falling on the film.
4. Film-holding system. Film can be taped to the back of a pinhole camera or loaded into a normal camera in a cassette, cartridge, or roll film. Light must be kept off it entirely until it is in position and ready to expose.
5. Viewfinder. At its simplest, a sighting mechanism.

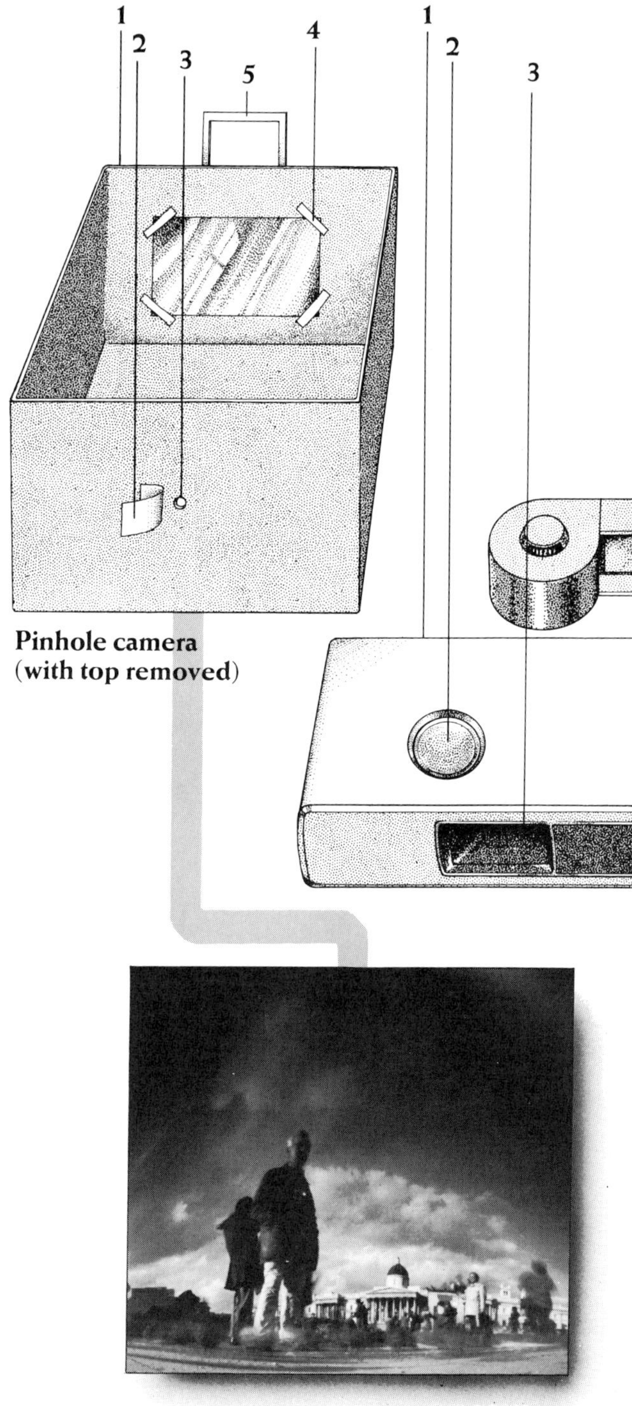

Pinhole camera (with top removed)

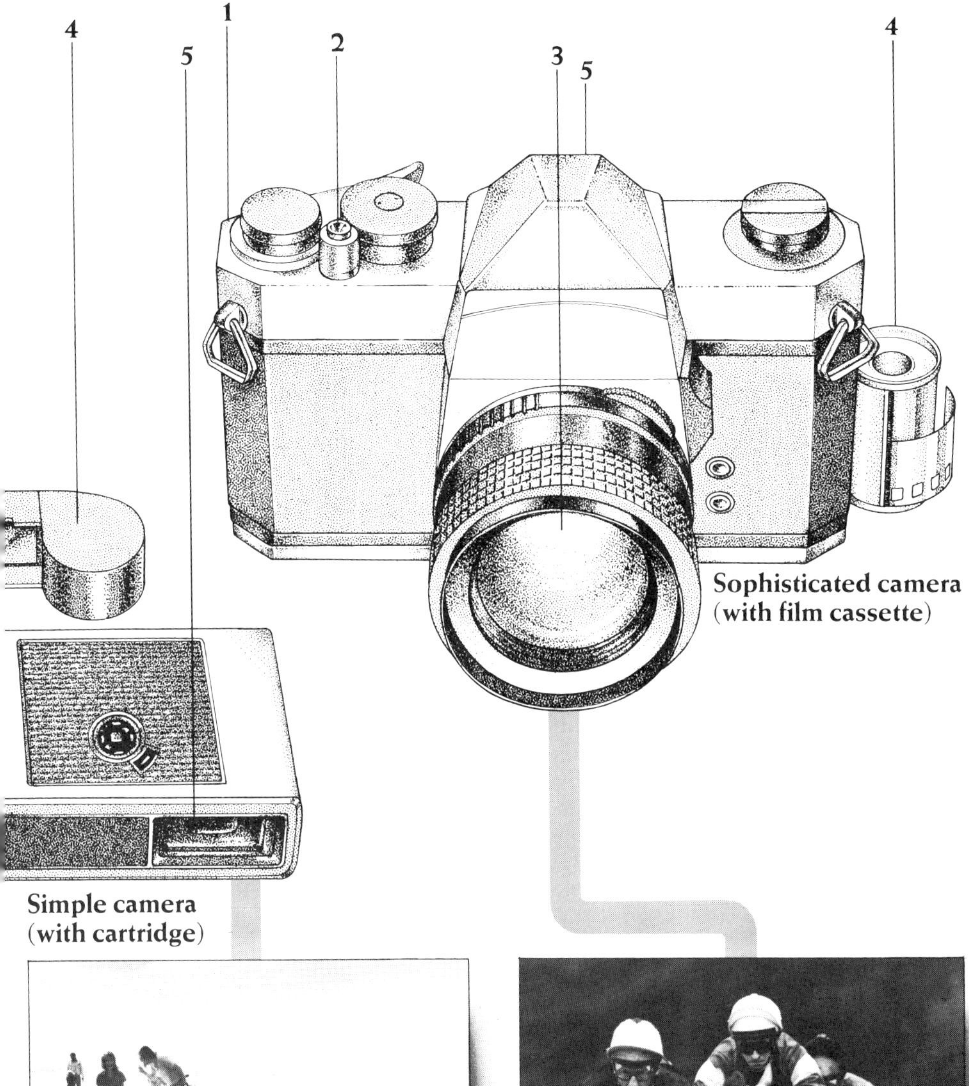

Sophisticated camera
(with film cassette)

Simple camera
(with cartridge)

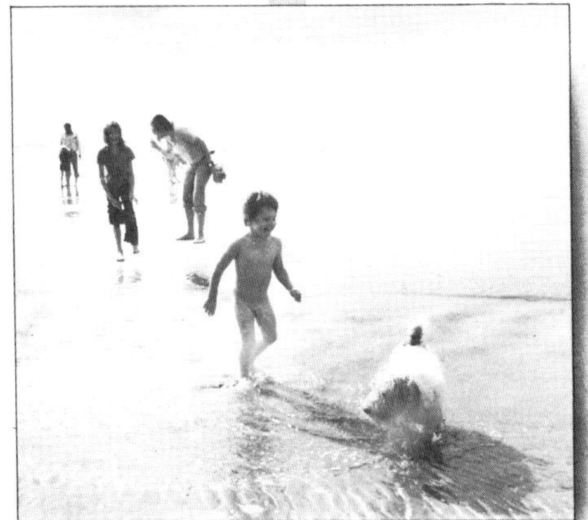

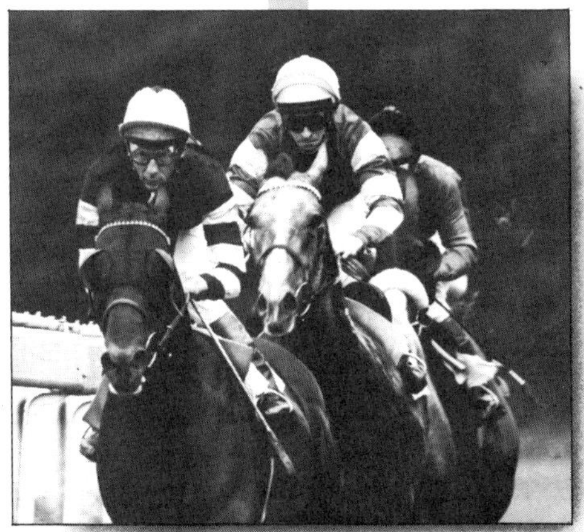

THE ETERNAL TRIANGLE
Aperture — shutter speed — focusing

The word *photography* means roughly, "light drawing." Light must fall on the film to make the exposure: not too little, not too much. Too little and there is hardly any effect: too much and the film becomes saturated with light.

When the shutter opens an image is thrown onto the film by the lens. If that image is very bright it should only be projected for a very short time, for example, a thousandth of a second. If the image is very weak it needs a longer time, perhaps a whole second. The exact time will also be influenced by the "speed" of the film. A film with a higher speed will react faster and therefore needs a shorter exposure time.

Obviously, the image on the film will be brighter if the light on the subject is brighter (for example on a bright day), and weaker if the subject is photographed indoors. But the brightness is also affected by the amount of light that the lens allows to pass. This is controlled by the aperture or diaphragm, a set of blades inside the lens which form a roughly circular opening that can be made bigger or smaller. As it is made bigger, more light gets through. For mathematical reasons the size of the hole is expressed in a rather complicated set of numbers: f/1.4, f/2, f/2.8, f/4, f/5.6, f/8, f/11, f/16, f/22. F/1.4 is the largest aperture; f/22 is the smallest. F/1.4 allows twice as much light through as f/2, and so on.

Thus, for any given brightness of the subject, there is a variety of ways the camera can be set to give the correct exposure: a lot of light for a short time, or a little light for a long time, or anything in between. For example, the correct exposure for Kodachrome 64 film on a dull day might be either 1/1000 of a second at f/2 (a large aperture, giving a bright image, for a very short time) or 1/15 of a second at f/16 (a very small aperture for a long time), or anything in between.

Exposure time

Aperture

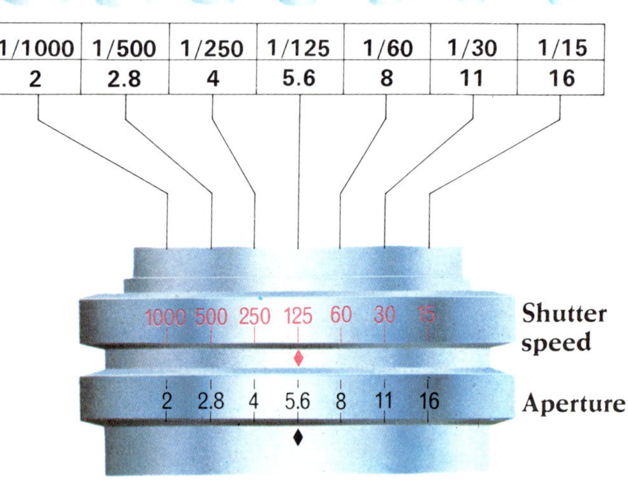

1/1000	1/500	1/250	1/125	1/60	1/30	1/15
2	2.8	4	5.6	8	11	16

Choosing the combination

If every combination of shutter speed and aperture gives the same exposure, why the complication? The problem is that the large apertures — f/2, f/2.8, etc., give a very shallow depth of field and make focusing more difficult; while at the other end of the scale, long shutter speed times allow for camera shake or subject movement problems.

To be sure of avoiding camera shake, the slowest practical shutter speed is 1/30, but 1/125 is much safer. For most pictures, set the shutter speed at 1/125 and the aperture according to the light conditions, as shown by your exposure meter or exposure chart.

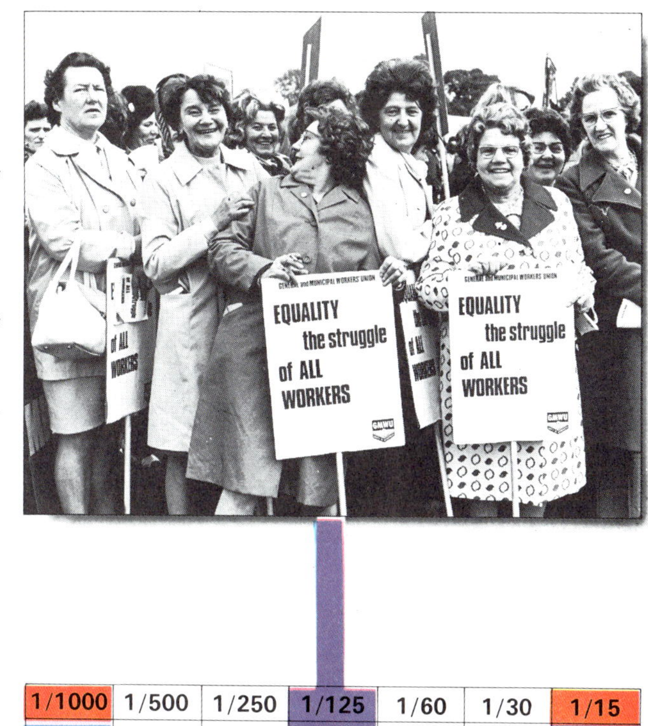

1/1000	1/500	1/250	1/125	1/60	1/30	1/15
2	2.8	4	5.6	8	11	16

1

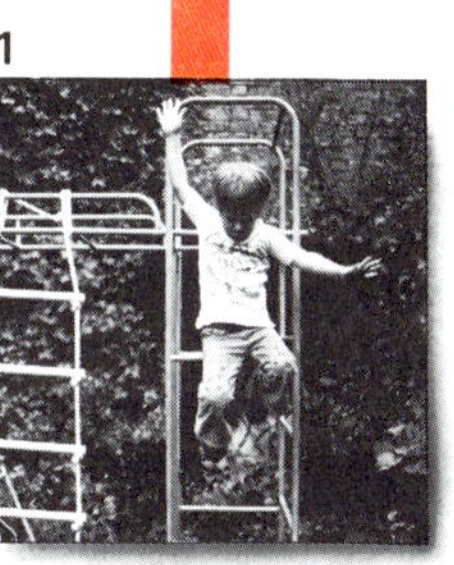

2

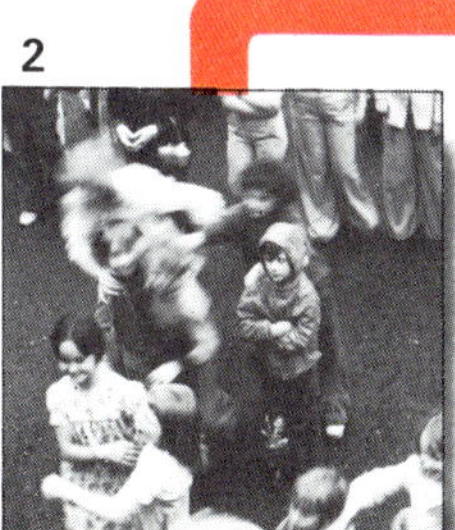

3

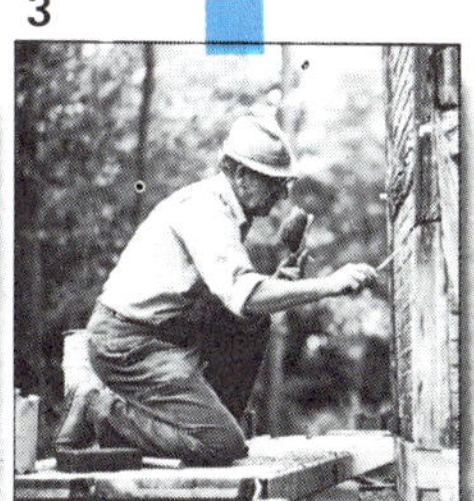

4

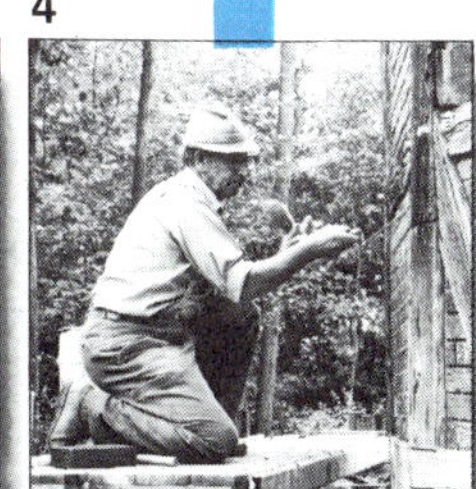

Exceptions

1. To freeze a fast moving subject. Move to the left on the above sample scale, using a faster shutter speed.

2. To blur a moving subject. For example, to give an increased sense of movement, select a slow shutter speed and set the appropriate aperture, e.g., 1/30 sec. at f/11.

3. To blur a complicated background (or foreground) by having it out of focus, choose a large aperture, for example f/2.

4. To get more of your subject sharp, behind and in front of where you focus, choose a small aperture, for example f/16.

Depth of field

This is the amount of the subject behind and in front of the point the camera is focused on, which is sharp. Smaller apertures give greater depth of field. As you focus closer you get less depth of field. Wide-angle (short focal length) lenses have more depth of field at the same aperture and distance than long focus lenses. It all sounds very complicated, and it is, if you try to learn it by heart right away. Instead, try forgetting all but the basic ideas outlined on these pages, and concentrate initially on the more important questions of picture-taking, such as what you want the picture to show.

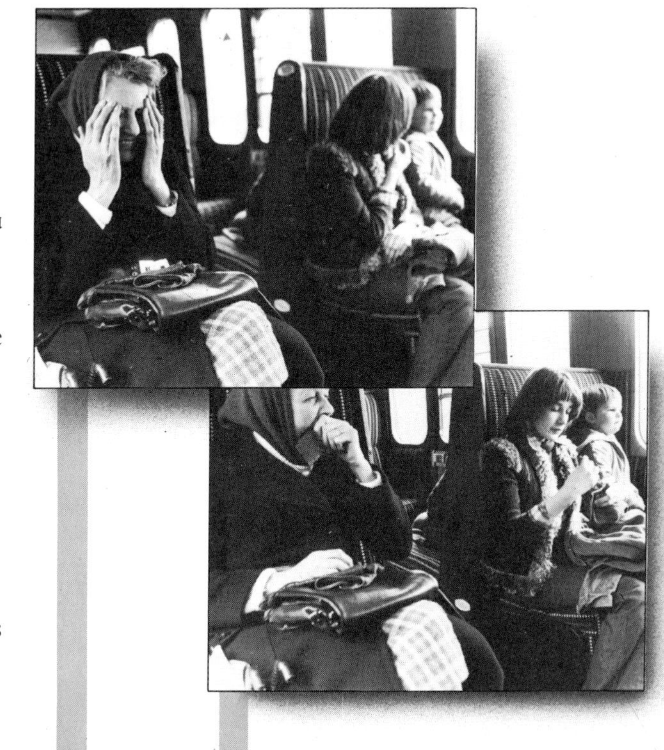

1/1000	1/500	1/250	1/125	1/60	1/30	1/15			
			2	2.8	4	5.6	8	11	16

Poor light

When you take pictures indoors you are unlikely to have the luxury of being able to use a shutter speed of 1/125, as room lighting will often require an aperture of f/1.4 or f/2, which many lenses do not have. In any case it is usually better to stop down a bit, that is, to choose a combination such as 1/30 at f/4. Although you will have to hold the camera still and squeeze the shutter release gently and smoothly in order to avoid camera shake, you will probably gain on balance as more of the picture will be in focus.

				1/1000	1/500	1/250	1/125	1/60	1/30	1/15
2	2.8	4	5.6	8	11	16				

Very bright light

The question of choosing the best combination of shutter speed and aperture effectively ceases to exist in very bright conditions, especially if you have a fast film in the camera. Whether you choose 1/1000 at f/8 (even assuming your camera has such a high shutter speed) or 1/250 at f/16, is often rather academic. If you do want to use a slow shutter speed to blur a moving subject, or a large aperture to throw a background out of focus, you will have to put a "neutral density" filter over the lens.

Controversies

As in many other areas of work, there are various debates and controversies current in the photographic world. Some of these are left over from earlier generations, some are about what kinds of photography are valid and useful, some about techniques, and others are about ethics.

Arguments about technique have often flared up but most of them center on camera format and make ("Can you get good quality on a toy like a 35 mm camera?") or developing and printing systems and formulas. One current argument is about the relative merits of black and white and color, but the questions raised are rarely technical. Opinions differ over which is more "real." Is black and white more abstract? Why is so much serious documentary work done on black and white? Does color offer more information or is the information inaccurate?

The most serious differences among photographers concern the relationship between form and content, ethical considerations in photographing other people, and the monetary value of photographic prints.

Form and content

Form and content are inextricably linked in a photograph, but different types of photographers will often stress one rather than the

▼ *Security guards outside a bank in Nairobi, Kenya, try to prevent their pictures from being taken.*

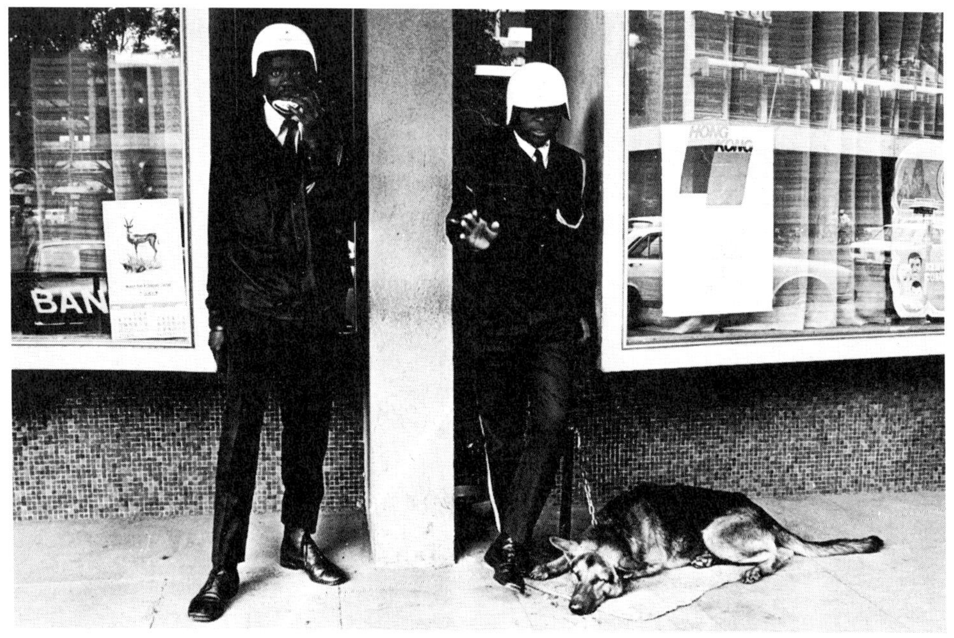

other. Pictorialists are mainly concerned with the beauty of the photographic image — its special qualities. Photojournalists and documentary photographers are mainly concerned with the content of a picture — what is being said.

Even within these general classifications there are splits. Is pictorialism art? What is realism? Does photography show the truth, one facet of the truth, or just an illusion? Many photographers believe that it is nearly impossible to give full information in one image. They don't believe in the single photographic print which distills reality, but think that photographs should be in series or sequences. This might be in the form of a traditional picture essay, a set of photographs on one or a chronologically related event.

Ethics

The main moral problems for photographers are about our right to photograph other people without their consent — especially if they are in a stressful situation — and how photographs obtained like this are used. War, grief, misery, and deprivation have been endlessly photographed. Do the photographs help to change or relieve situations or are they

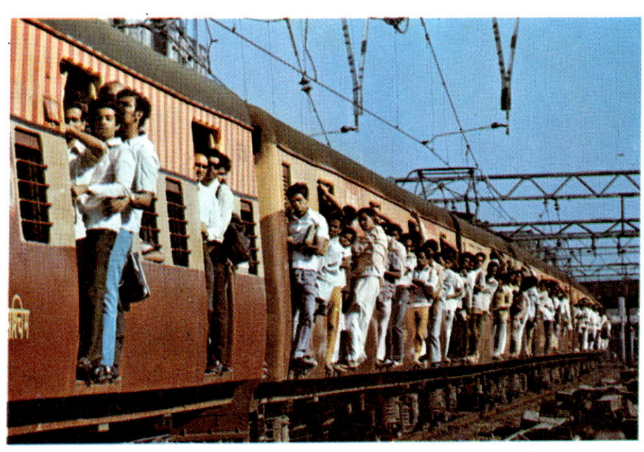

◀ *This scene of the morning rush hour in Bombay was photographed separately in b/w and color. Which version tells you more?*

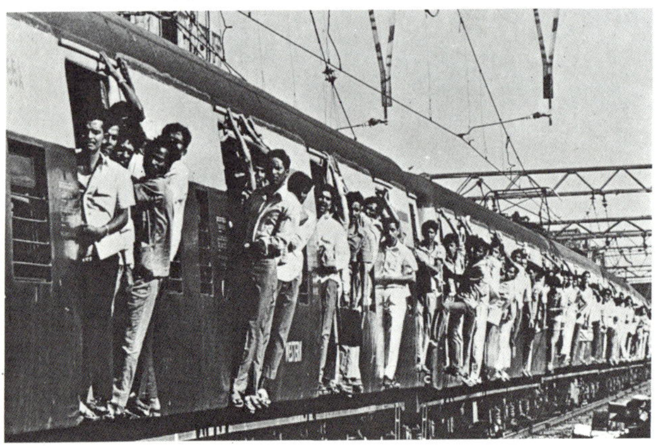

▶ *This portrait of Herschel is in an album of photographs by Julia Margaret Cameron that was sold at Sotheby's in 1974 for over $100,000 and is now in the National Portrait Gallery in London.*

only exploiting people for gain or personal kudos? Walter Benjamin, the German critic, first raised these questions in the 1930s but it is only now that photographers are beginning to consider them seriously.

Monetary values of photographs

And what about the economic value of a photographic print? Until the late 1960s photographic prints were considered to be cheap, reproducible images. With the rise in importance and cost of historical photographs, collectors began to take more interest in modern "masters." After prestigious auction sales of 19th century pictures in London and New York, art galleries began to show more and more photographic exhibitions. Signed prints by living photographers started to sell at prices between about $20 and $1000. But what are they? Originals? Not unless the negative is destroyed. Limited editions? Ditto. The other problem is that it is not only "pictorial" pictures which are hung in museums and galleries as high art. Often large blowups of war scenes and atrocities are shown in this way. What are we supposed to make of these photographs in this context? Are we being asked to view the form and ignore the content? Is that possible? The argument over whether photography is an art or a craft continues and is often reflected in people's attitudes to training photographers. Should students become apprentices, take a course at a technical college, or spend four years studying for a degree? Like many of the other questions in the photographic world, it depends on what you want to do and for whom you want to do it.

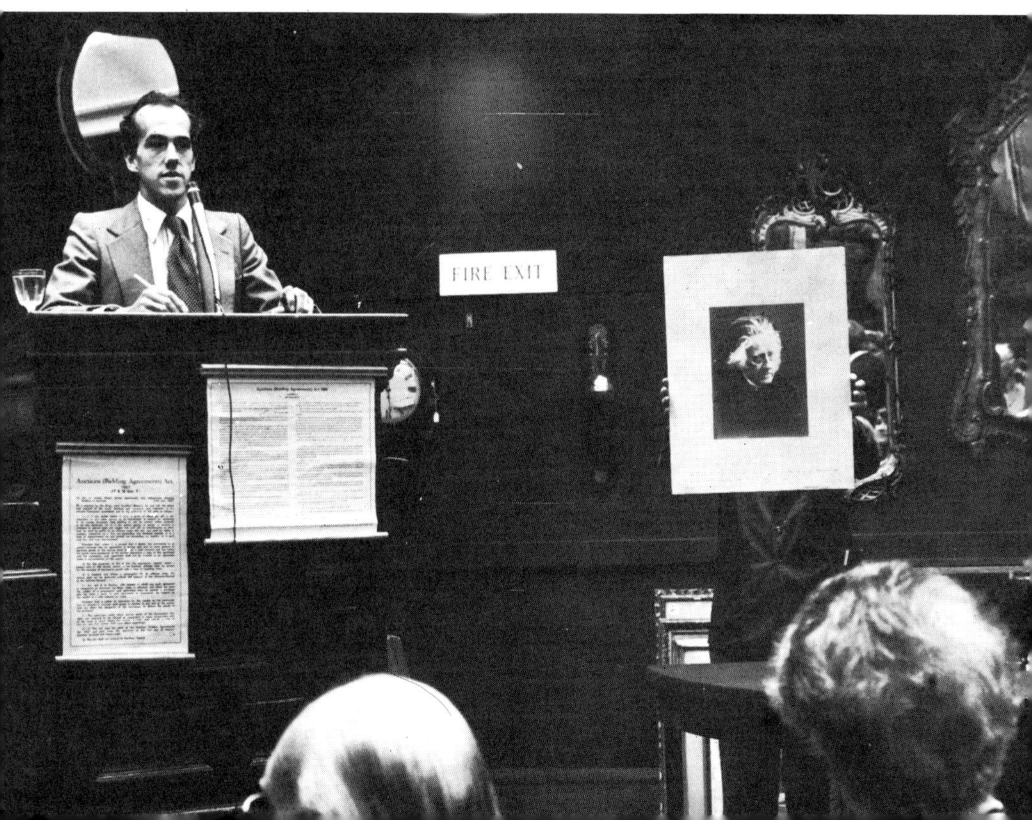

Art, history, and photography

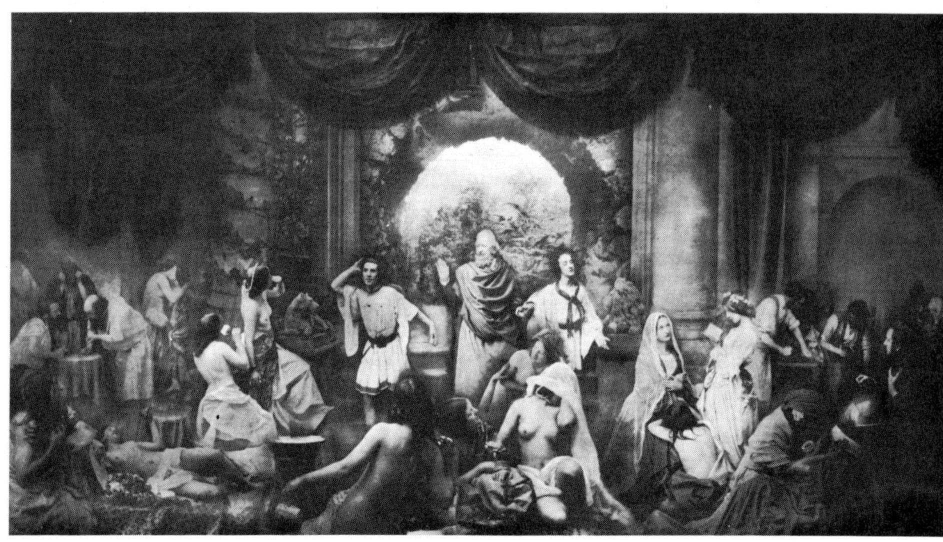

▲ *This montage of* Two Ways of Life *was made from 30 negatives and caused a scandal when it was first shown in 1856.*

Art has been defined in different ways in different cultures and historical periods. Photography's claim to be an art form has been hotly debated since its invention in the 19th century. It has never been wholly accepted as art by photographers or critics. Many have tried to prevent it being so classified, believing that its main importance is as a communication tool to record and represent the world.

Shortly after the birth of photography, Paul Delaroche proclaimed that "from today painting is dead." But photography did not kill painting. On the contrary, some of the most important artists and art movements of the 19th and 20th centuries were influenced and inspired by it. Photography itself split up almost immediately into two mainstreams. Commercial photography resulted in the boom in portrait studios and the sale of views from all over the world; and fine art photography simply tried to emulate the high art of the period. The aping of the 19th century's narrative or "realist" paintings was largely disastrous for photography, although individuals tried to find styles of their own, as did Julia Margaret Cameron.

Photography as art developed along diverging tracks in various parts of the world. In England, the two strands of nineteenth century romanticism and naturalism continued into the twentieth century. In the 1930s a new style of documentary and narrative photography began, appearing in news magazines like *Picture Post.* In Germany, photography and photomontage were used for political or social propaganda and many of the artists and designers at the Bauhaus used it as a means of self-expression or incorporated it in designs. The Dada and Surrealist movements in Europe produced many photographic images. Following the revolution in 1918, the Russian avant-garde viewed photography as

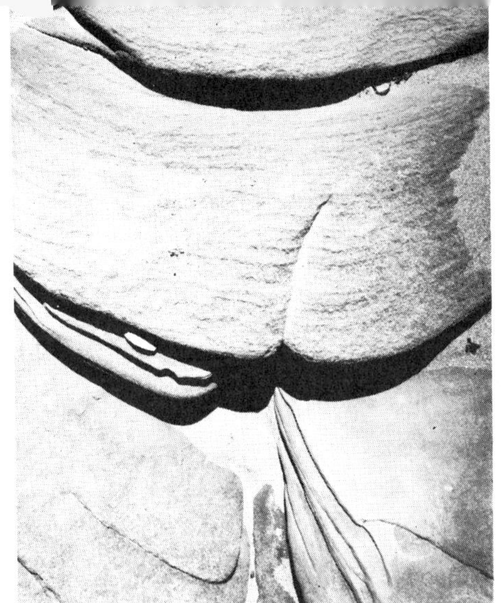

▲ *Much pictorialism concentrates on recording the beauty of natural forms.*

an important and powerful folk art and a tool of education and propaganda.

The turn of the century in the United States saw the birth of American pictorialism. Photographers like Edward Steichen concentrated on the beauty of nature and photographic forms and were very influenced by tradition in painting. Galleries were opened for photography and photo-art magazines started. This developed later into the incisive, technically perfect pictorialism of men like Edward Weston and Ansel Adams. Much of this work was considered art in its own time. During the Depression, a new school of documentary photography grew up, which included Walker Evans and Dorothea Lange. At the time their detailed and realistic representations of ordinary life were definitely not seen as art. Nowadays many of those documentary pictures, as well as the work of other documentary photographers, are shown in art museums and sold in galleries. They have become art.

In the 1960s and 1970s artists started to work with photographic images and techniques, for example, Pop Art. Conceptual artists have used photographs to express ideas and to question the validity and truth of photographic images themselves. Some criticize the whole art world as institutionalized and money-oriented. One conceptual photographer/artist, Victor Burgin, has said that photographers trying to be recognized by galleries and museums are like "people rowing out to join a sinking ship."

Maybe this attitude will help photography to become more self-reliant and prevent some of its practitioners from continually considering themselves the poor relations of the art world instead of independent operators in a much wider context.

▼ *Poster designed to go on show in the streets of Newcastle, by Victor Burgin.*

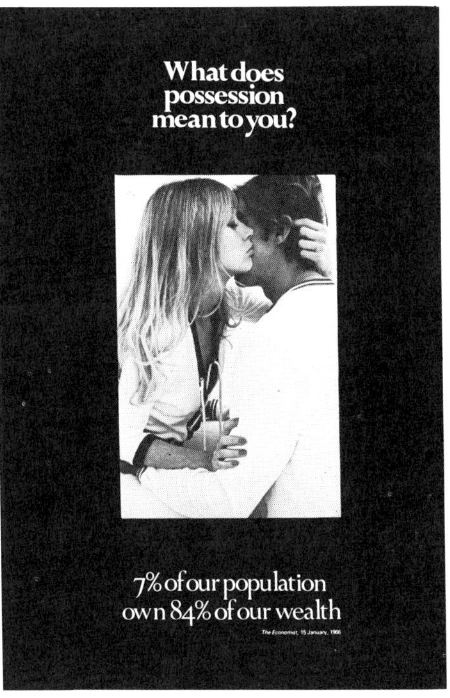

Alternative approaches

In the past few years, in many different countries, there has been a decided rejection of, or movement away from, some of the more traditional aspects and values of photography. This movement ranges from photojournalists who wish to have more control over the ways in which their work is used, to those who have photographic skills and want to work in groups or to see the skills employed more usefully (and less competitively) in their own communities.

Similarly some people are working toward the use of photography as an integral part of education, so that children can learn from an early age how to record their own lives while also learning how to understand visual symbols and the way in which photography is used in mass media. It is felt that this early demystification of technology in the acquisition of skills both in producing and decoding pictures will help children to be more questioning about media and its inherent values.

Some photographers have felt so strongly about having editorial control over their work that they have withdrawn from servicing newspapers at all. Some have even started their own picture agencies or cooperatives or have gone into publishing. For instance, Phillip Jones Griffiths spent two years working on the photography, text, and design of his book *Vietnam Inc.* so that he could portray matters as he understood them. Taking control of the entire process from beginning to end, he successfully produced a book that (even

▸ *Even at an early age children can learn how to record their own lives.*

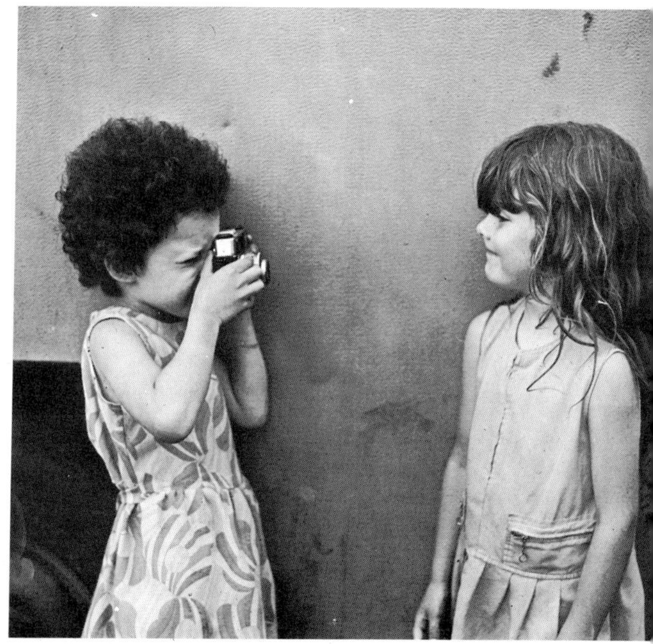

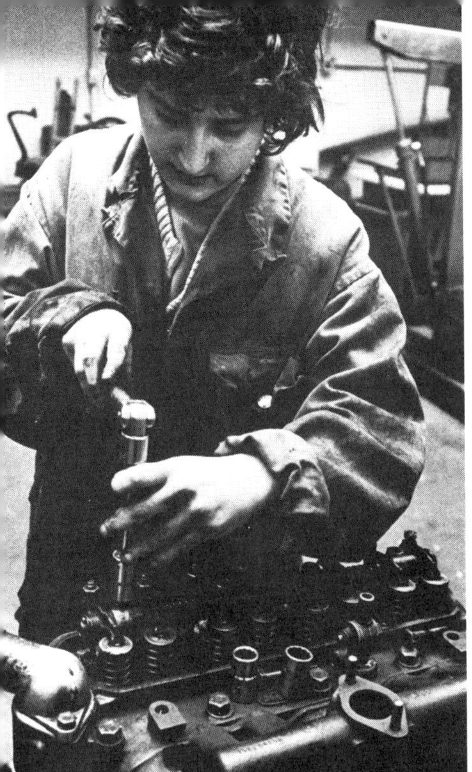

◀ *There is a photography organization that takes pictures in an effort to counteract the distorted and stereotyped view of women as portrayed in mass media.*

after the event) was able to put into a historical and political perspective some of the distorted accounts of what had really happened in Vietnam.

The best known agency that was begun by photographers as a cooperative is Magnum Photos, Inc. Magnum was founded in 1947 in New York City by Henri Cartier-Bresson, Robert Capa, George Rodger, and David Seymour.

Various ad hoc groups of photographers have also united to pool their thinking and skills in order to document particular areas of conflict or social change about which they feel strongly. This group activity has also been found to be a most efficient way to produce photographs quickly, with the emphasis on joint effort, rather than individualistic whims. One such British group abandoned all other work while they traveled to major cities in Britain, taking photographs, collecting statistics, and conducting interviews and attitude polls, culminating in their traveling exhibition "Problem in the City." This raised vital issues about town planning blight and the gulf between bureaucrats and their knowledge of the real needs of people.

Another group of photographers, in New York City, set themselves the task of documenting Puerto Rican life in that city.

In addition to such groups, many individual photographers are involved in documenting society. A collection of such photos is in the book *The Concerned Photographer.*

In their spare time, women in another group of photographers are gradually recording a photographic and statistical view of women's working and social lives in Hackney, London. This is in an effort to counteract the stereotyped and (in their opinion) totally distorted picture of women as depicted in mass media. Their photographs are used regularly in local schools, in community groups.

Numerous others are fighting for the meager funds available from charities, foundations, government and private bodies, and photographic companies, to document a variety of projects. These range from homelessness in inner cities, to pollution and the changing face of the land.

Some photographers and galleries are also tired of the traditional system of merely putting pictures up on walls and allowing them "to speak for themselves." One recent departure from this well-known cliché is the International Center of Photography in New York City. The ICP has regular gallery shows, and often the shows are integrated with seminars on the photographers' work.

In addition, the ICP has a program of workshops, lectures, and courses. Many of the

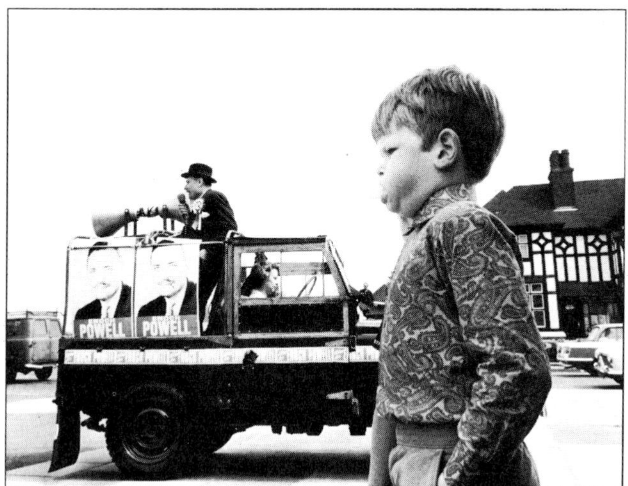

◀ *One of the "Real Britain" series of postcards, an independent venture by a photographic cooperative to show another view of England.*

courses have been evaluated by New York University and some can be taken for credit at the undergraduate and graduate levels. The ICP is concerned with all phases of photography.

There is also a major move toward the use of photography in education. Several strands have emerged, covering such diverse areas as identity and photo-literacy (learning to read and write by taking and producing photographs, then telling, recording, and eventually writing down stories about the pictures taken). One youth project using photography with their eight to seventeen year-olds can now boast that newcomers to the group are out in the street taking photographs twenty minutes after joining the project.

Another approach to photography is to encourage groups of children to use exploratory techniques. They usually start with simple pinhole cameras so that an understanding of how an image is formed without even using a lens becomes the basis and principle on which to build further work. Using simple technology, children can then travel along the same route as that through which photography itself evolved. This helps to encourage creativity.

Others are working toward group interaction and self-discovery via the use of cameras, using photo-games, or preparing identity books for themselves. Photography is often used by art teachers inside schools and is also being investigated as a form of therapy.

A new breed of photographers, based within neighborhoods, is also slowly defining the role they can play in passing on skills, helping people to document or record their own lives and needs. Tenants' associations, for instance, often use photography to campaign for better housing conditions. People can then be more involved in decision making about their own lives, instead of waiting for things to change. There also are faint signs that those who would formerly have joined a camera club — renowned for their slide battles and competitive endeavors — will also drift toward being more community-oriented. Some clubs are again involved in recording their towns and villages for local history or amenity groups in the way they were in the nineteenth century.

Photographers are also going into the business of self-publishing. One group, with their "Real Britain" series of postcards, borrowed money in order to finance a publication project that brought together a diversity of photographers to combine and present a unique set of picture postcards. Breaking away forever from dull views of towns and resorts, they approached shops and galleries directly with their "real" view of Britain.

This trend can also be seen in the United States. In many cases, books are published by individuals. But it often happens that a small, little-known publishing company will print books that otherwise would not get published. One can find these companies by a trip to a bookstore that stocks a fair number of photography books.

Alongside the progress of an alternative photography movement a whole series of alternative magazines and newspapers has also developed. These are encouraging new types of photojournalism, not linked to the needs of advertisers (from whom a major part of funding comes in mass circulation publications), but considering the needs of readers.

All these ideas and trends constitute a major shift away from the entrenched attitudes held in most colleges and professional bodies, written about in journals, and encouraged by major photographic manufacturers, which see photography only in terms of sales of materials or equipment. Fortunately alternative phototechnology is also now being investigated in an effort to prevent some of the finer craft aspects of photography from vanishing entirely.

▼ *Marc Riboud — Japan. Traditional rally of amateur photographers.*

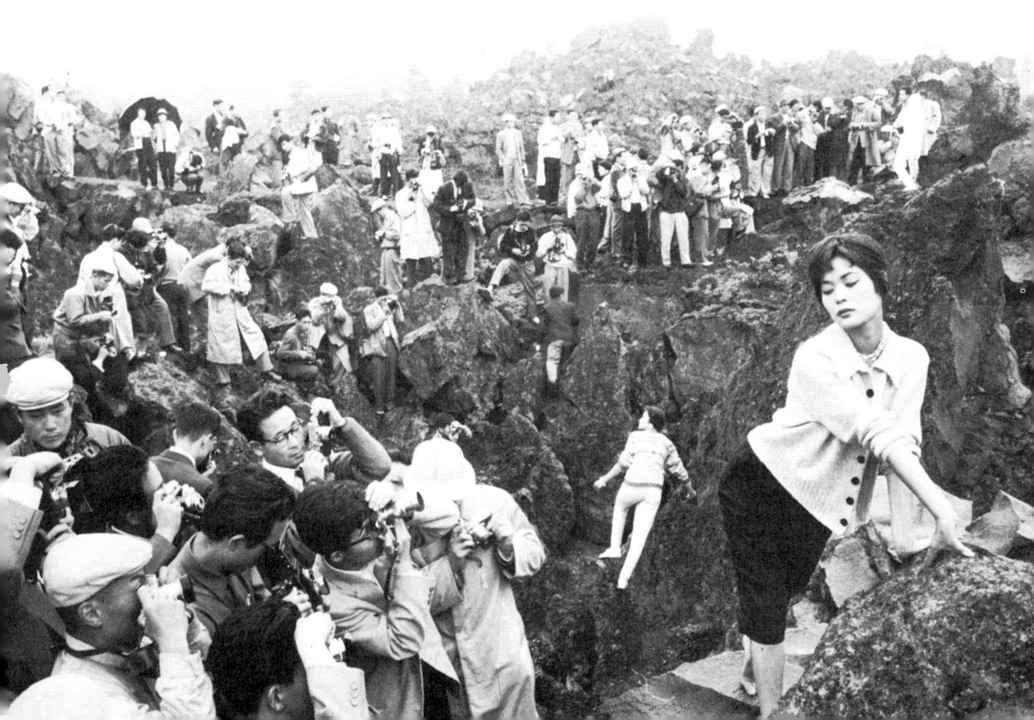

The photographic process

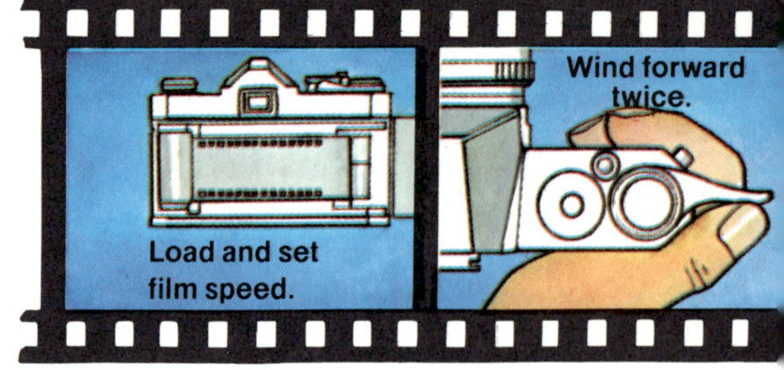

This chart shows in simplified form the steps involved in shooting and processing a black and white picture. It serves as a contents listing for the activities section and can also be used in other ways. First, it can help you to gain an overall idea of the photographic process, and second, it can be used as a check list or reminder when you start practical work.

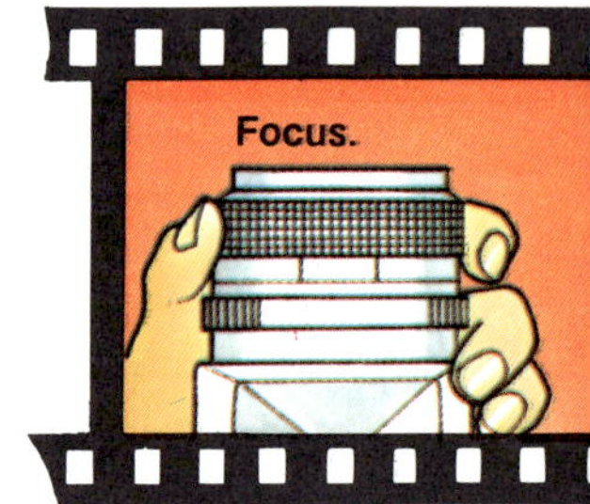

...find a darkroom.

Take film from cassette, cartridge, or separate from backing paper.

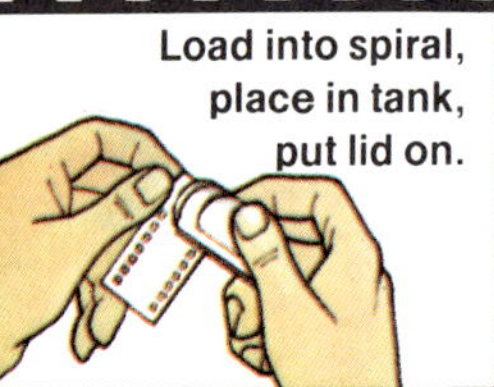

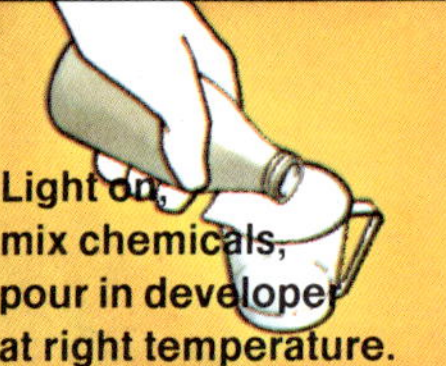

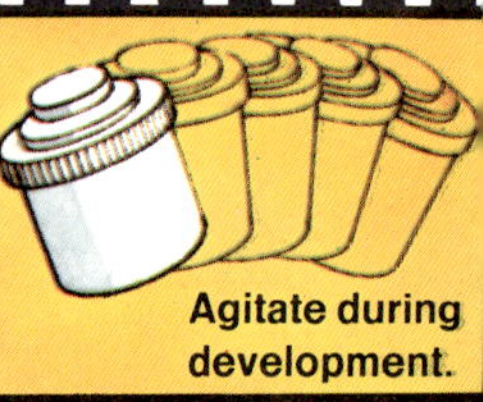

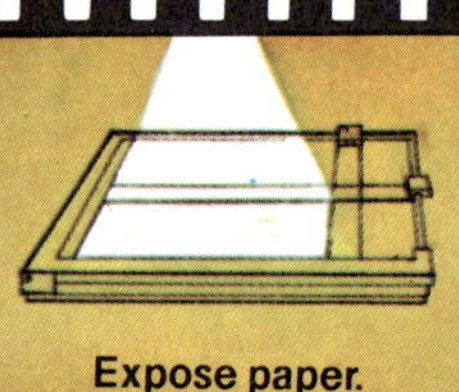

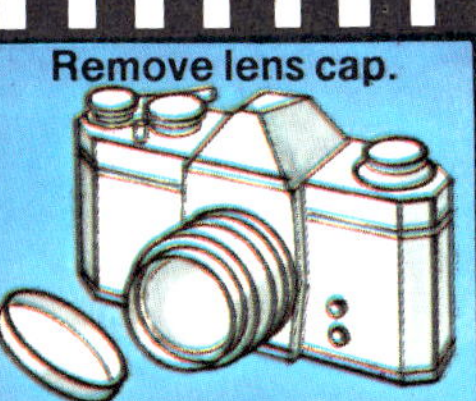
Remove lens cap.

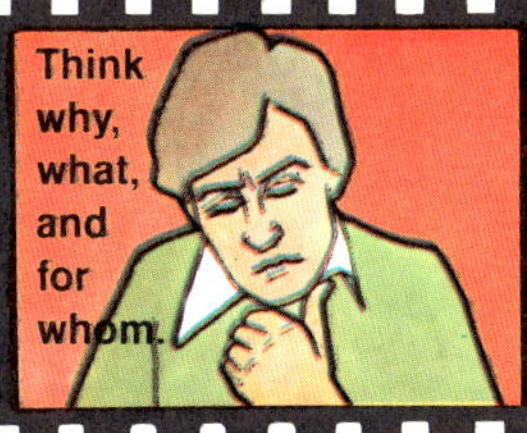
Think
why,
what,
and
for
whom.

Use flash if needed.
M or X setting.

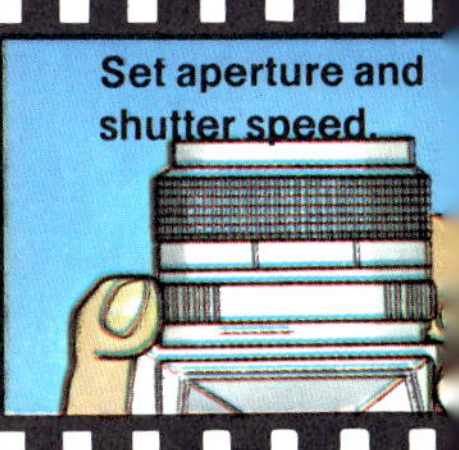
Set aperture and
shutter speed.

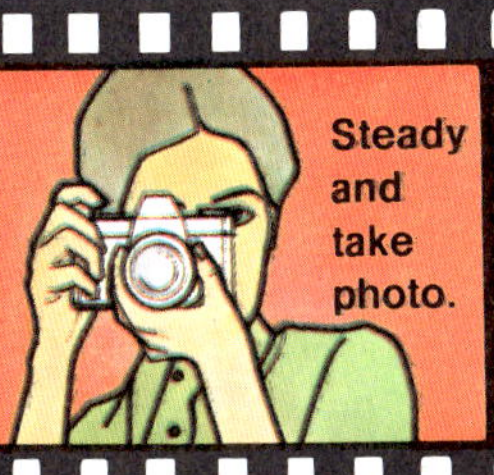
Steady
and
take
photo.

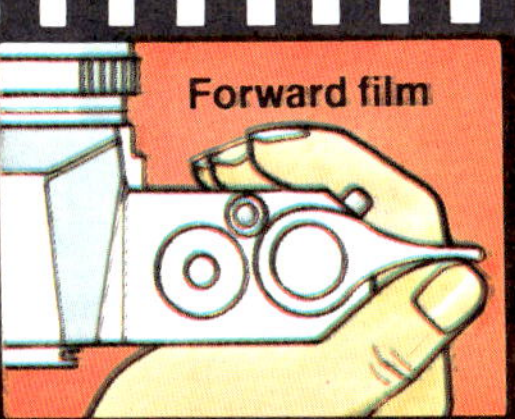
Forward film

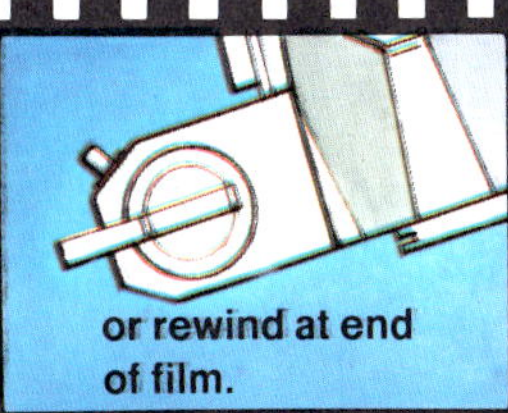
or rewind at end
of film.

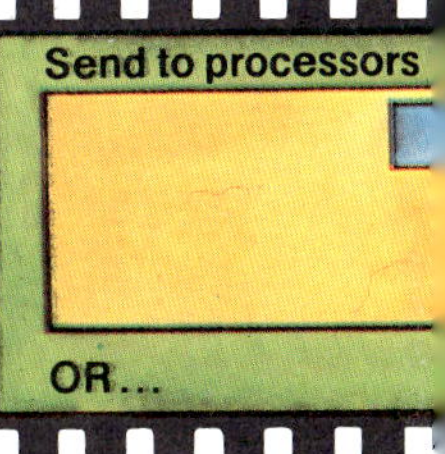
Send to processors
OR…

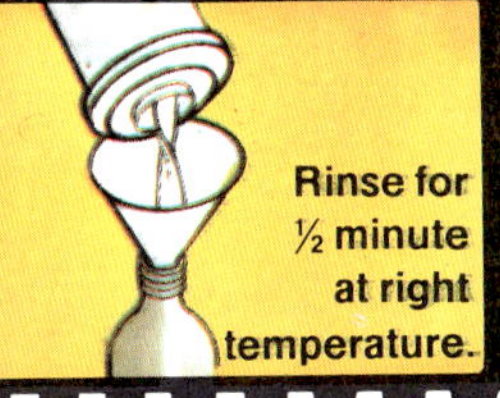
Rinse for
½ minute
at right
temperature.

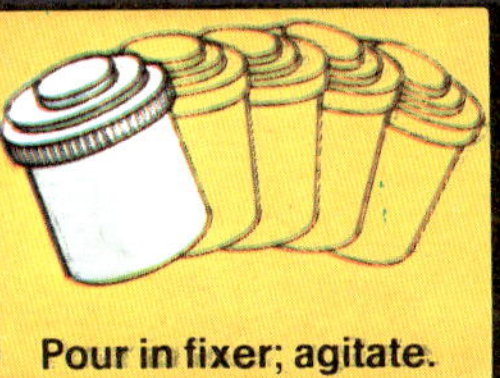
Pour in fixer; agitate.

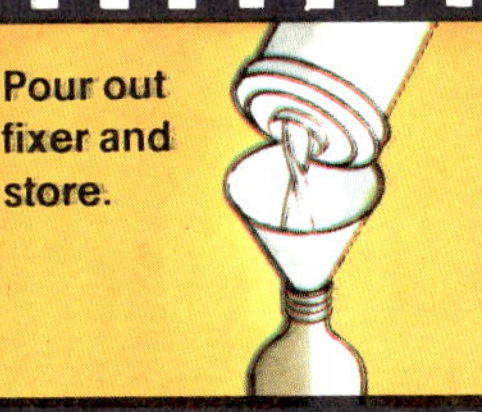
Pour out
fixer and
store.

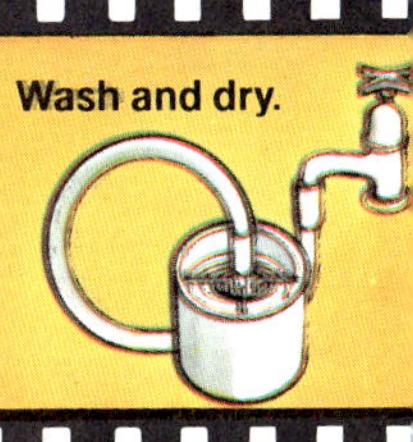
Wash and dry.

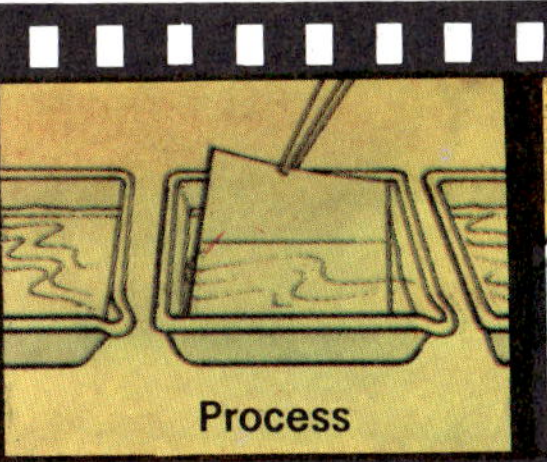
Process

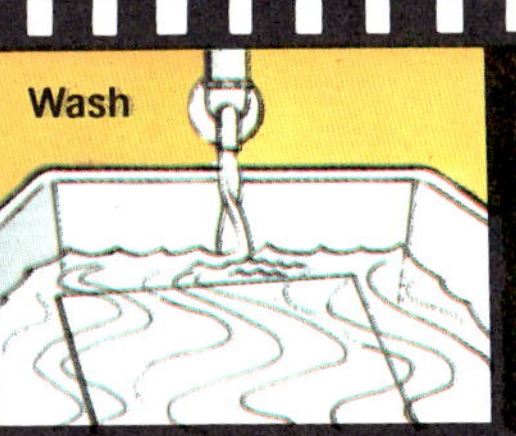
Wash

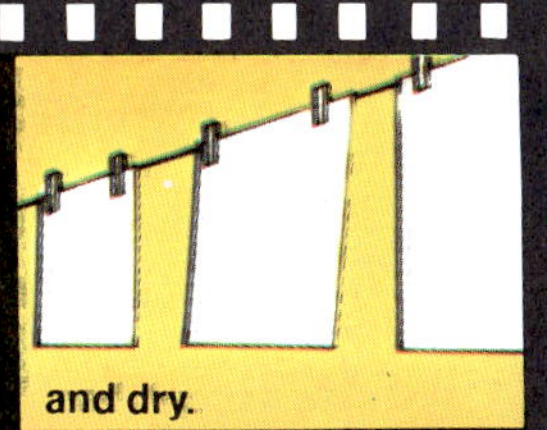
and dry.

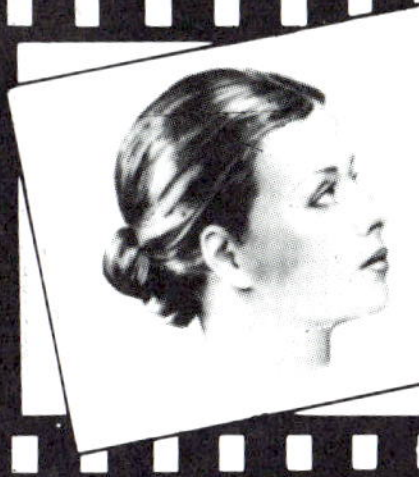

Basic camera types

There are many variations on these basic types and many versions of each type. Prices are usually dependent on quality: the accuracy of the engineering, special features, and particularly the sharpness and maximum aperture of the lens. For example an inexpensive pocket camera has a pressed plastic body with a single element plastic lens, while a Rollei SL66 costing more than $1,000 has a practically hand-built, complex metal body and a six element glass lens. There are also cameras designed for specialized use, like plate or underwater cameras, and a range of attachments to extend the versatility of any model.

Viewfinding mechanisms

Simple viewfinder camera

The image formed by the taking lens falls on the film and exposes it when the shutter is fired. The viewfinder is also a simple lens that is designed to show approximately the same view of the subject as the taking lens. Film is loaded into the back of the camera in a sealed cartridge or a roll.

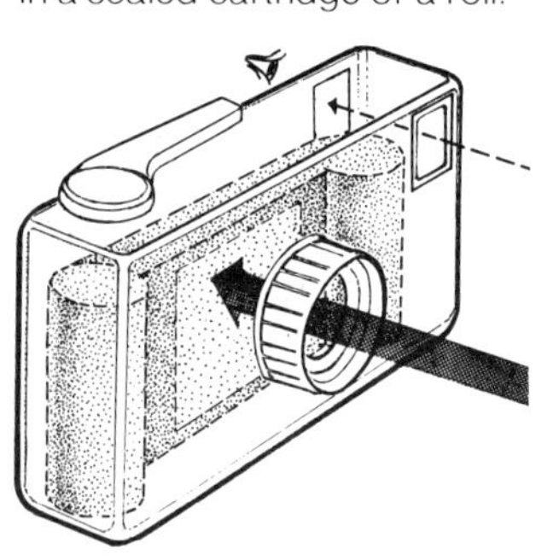

Rangefinder

35 mm. rangefinder cameras have an accurate viewfinder giving virtually the same image as the taking lens. It is coupled with a built-in rangefinder that shows in the viewfinder when the chosen subject is in focus.

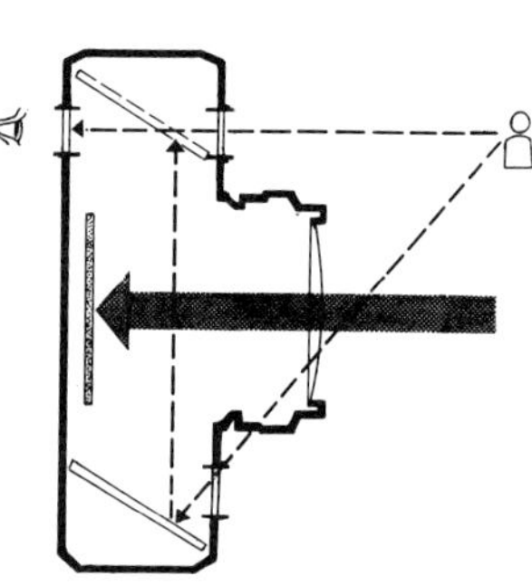

Twin lens reflex (TLR)

Usually a 2¼" square (negative size) camera. This has two matched lenses. One forms the viewfinder image and the other, mounted below it, a nearly identical image that is thrown onto the film when the shutter is fired. The camera usually is loaded with roll film.

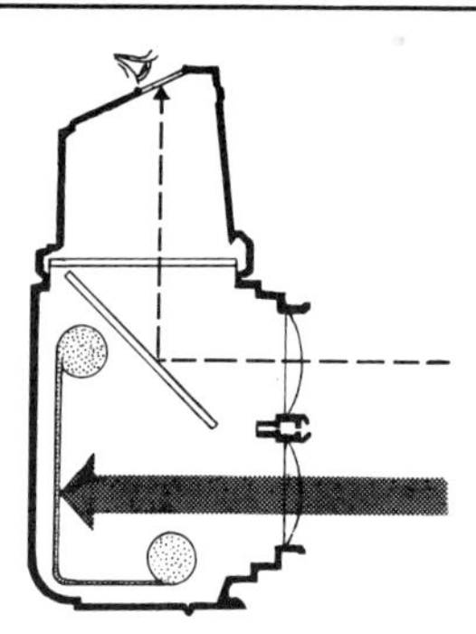

Single lens reflex (SLR)

You see exactly the same image in the viewfinder as falls on the film, by having a mirror at 45° in front of the film that reflects the image from the lens into the viewfinder. When the shutter is released it flicks up momentarily to allow exposure of the film. Viewing is coupled to focusing.

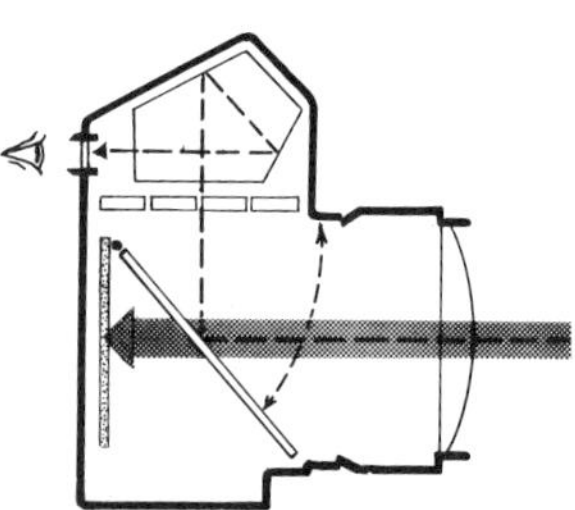

CHOICES

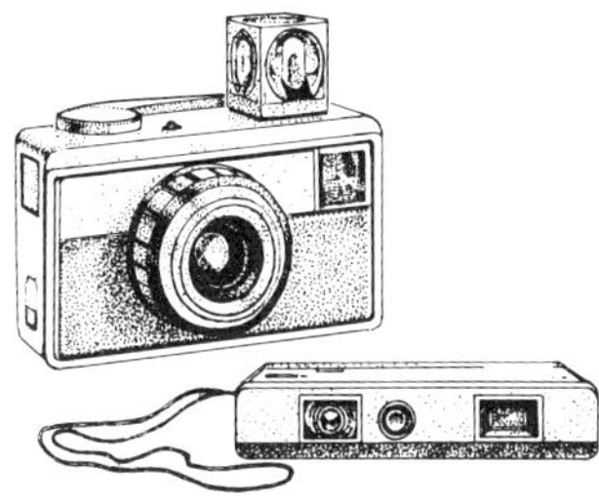

Simple camera
110 film. Cheap and very easy to use. Good for static subjects in good light. Ideal for snaps which do not have to be greatly enlarged. Usually fixed focus and choice of symbol f/nos. Direct viewfinder. Some take flash cubes. Cartridges usually sent away for processing.

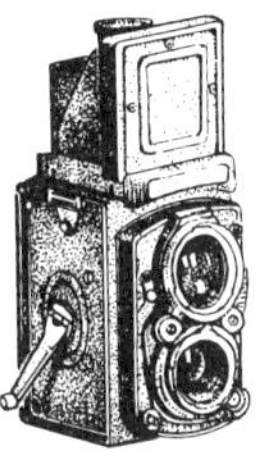

2¼ square TLR
Roll film (pictures 6cm x 6 cm). Can be expensive. High quality results because of large negative/transparency size. Slower to use than 35mm and not so good for action. Good for portraits, scenes, etc. Range of shutter speeds and f/nos. Large viewfinder with coupled focusing (viewfinder image from upper lens). Parallax problems. Usually noninterchangeable lenses. Bulb and electronic flash.

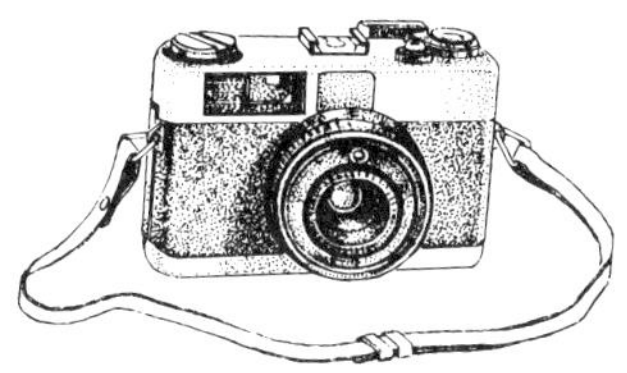

Simple 35mm
35mm film cassettes. Relatively cheap. Can photograph some moving subjects. Often symbol settings for f/nos. shutter speeds, and focusing. Limited exposure range but sometimes automatic control. Direct viewfinder. Noninterchangeable lens. Usually takes bulb and electronic flash. Small negatives require careful processing and printing.

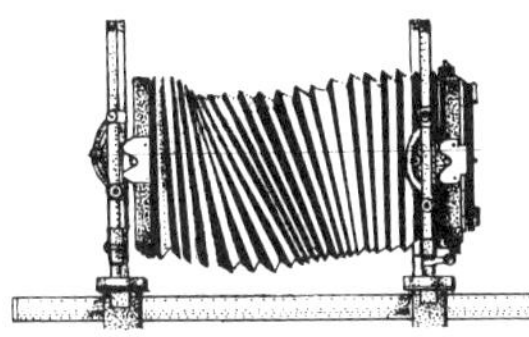

Plate cameras
Single exposure of cut film up to 8 in. x 10 in. Expensive to buy, slow and difficult to use. Must be fixed to tripod. Superb technical quality. Ideal for professional studio sets and architecture. Numerous lenses and gadgets.

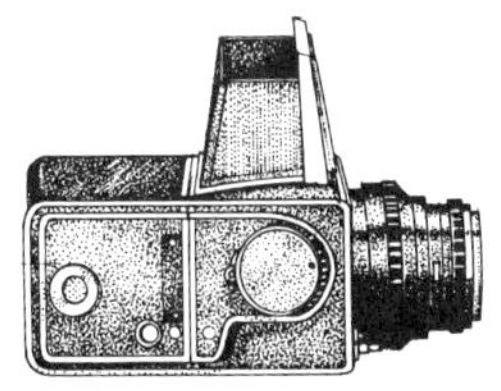

2¼ square SLR
Roll film (pictures 6 cm x 6 cm). Usually very expensive. High quality on large negative. Bulky and slow to use. Often kept for studio work or location set-up where a tripod can be used. Full exposure range (nonautomatic). Accurate, couple focusing through taking lens. Interchangeable lenses and film backs. Bulb and electronic flash.

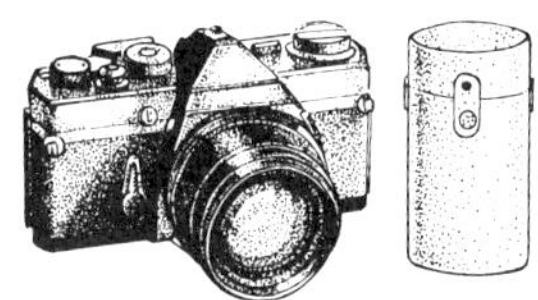

Sophisticated 35mm
35mm film cassettes. Can be very expensive. Versatile, complex to use properly. Suitable for all types of moving subjects in good or bad lighting. Wide exposure range — coupled and/or automatic. Accurate, coupled focusing by rangefinder or through the lens. Wide range of interchangeable lenses and additional equipment to extend use, e.g., for microscopy. Bulb and electronic flash. Small negatives require great care in processing.

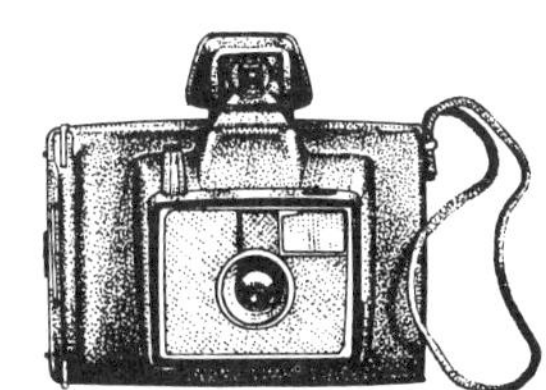

Instant picture
Special film. Finished prints in about 10 seconds (b/w), 60 seconds (color). Prints expensive. Variety of exposure and focusing systems. Noninterchangeable lenses. Direct viewfinder. Bulb and electronic flash.

Lenses

Normal lens
Same distance from subject.

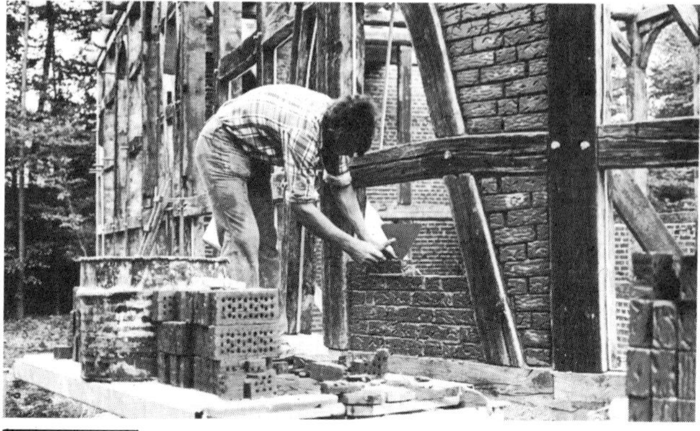

Long-focus lens
Same distance from subject.

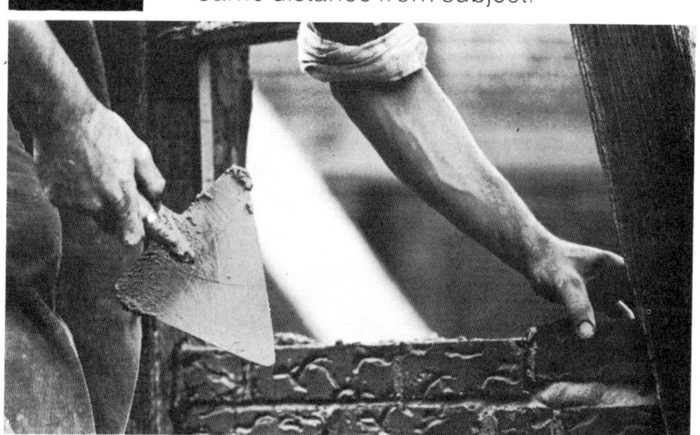

Wide-angle lens
Same distance from subject.

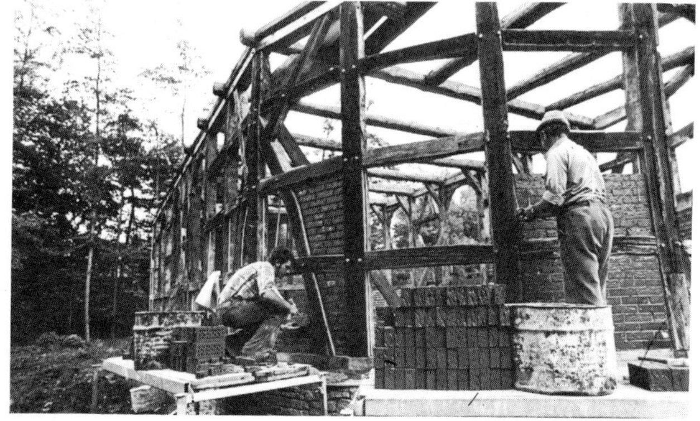

Most cameras have a "normal" lens (built in or changeable). The three pictures on this page were taken from the same position using a normal, long-focus (telephoto), and wide-angle lens. Compared to the normal lens, the long-focus picture covers less of the subject, and gives a shallower depth of field (the background is blurred). The wide-angle picture includes more of the scene and has more depth of field (the aperture is the same throughout). There is no other difference. The perspective stays the same because the viewpoint is the same.

By contrast, the three pictures on the opposite page have been taken at varying distances so that the bricklayer stays roughly the same size. Depth of field is as before, but notice that the perspective changes, as the viewpoint has been changed. The perspective of the long-focus shot has been flattened and compressed. Elements in the background are scarcely smaller than similar elements in the foreground; the row of bricks being laid looks shorter. In the wide-angle shot the perspective has become steeper; background elements are made smaller (you get more background in); and the row of bricks seems longer. (The lenses used here were 55mm, 200mm and 24mm.)

Normal lens
Subject kept same size, distance 3 m.

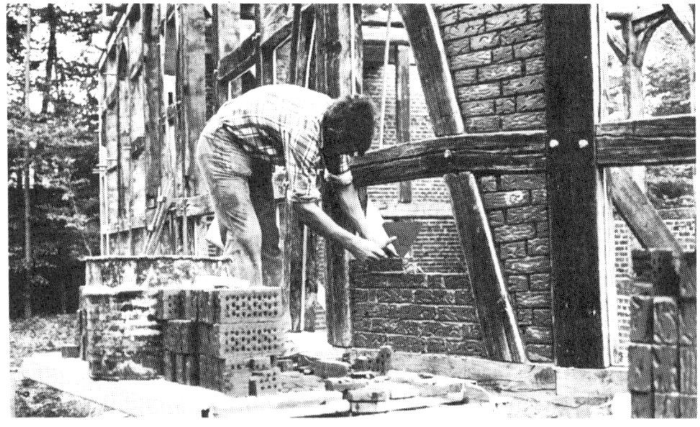

Long-focus lens
Subject kept same size, distance 10 m.

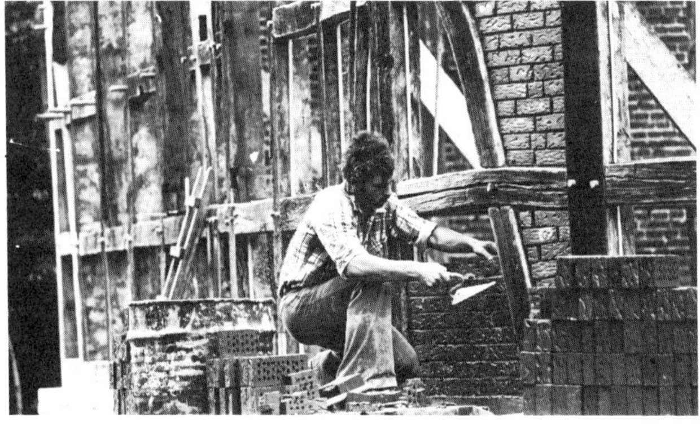

Wide-angle lens
Subject kept same size, distance 1 m.

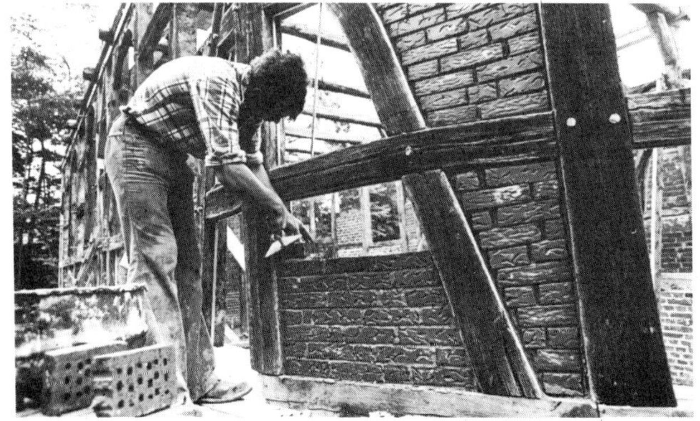

Taking care of the lens

The lens must be kept clean, but is easily scratched. First blow dust or grit off. Use a puffer-brush or jet of air, (or blow hard) then wipe smears and fingerprints (deadly) with a lens-cleaning tissue or soft clean cloth. Keep a lens cap on when not in use.

Lens hoods help to avoid *flare* (washing out of the image by extraneous light), keep rain off the lens, and help protect the lens against fingerprints. Use them especially on a dull day.

Filters

A *filter* is a piece of glass or plastic that modifies the light as it enters the camera.

U.V. or 1a filters protect the lens from fingerprints and cut down the blue haze that occurs in distance shots.

Yellow, orange, or red filters are for black and white photography and are used mainly to darken the sky and show up clouds.

Polarizing filters cut down certain reflections and can darken the sky if you are shooting at about 90° to the sun. Use with color or b/w.

Color correction (cc) filters come in different strengths of different colors. These are mainly for specialized work but 20 Magenta helps correct green cast from fluorescent lighting (it varies) while 05 Yellow warms up flash or gray-day shots.

Soft focus filters make the picture look romantic.

Taking the picture

Before taking a photograph with any camera there are four related operations to perform. On certain modern cameras some of these operations are automatic. They are: 1. Set the film speed; 2. Load the camera; 3. Calculate and set the correct f/no. and shutter speed (exposure); and 4. Focus. On most modern cameras it is preferable to use a lens hood to prevent flare, whether the sun is shining or not.

Set the film speed according to the speed ratings that are printed on every film box, usually as ASA or DIN settings. (In the ASA system doubling the number doubles the film speed, e.g., 400 ASA is twice as fast as 200 ASA. In the DIN system an increase of 3 doubles the speed, e.g., 30 DIN is double the speed of 27 DIN). Faster films will record in lower light levels but they lose in photographic quality. Tear off the side of the film box that has this information and keep it with the camera to remind you of the film speed and type you have loaded. Set the film speed on your built-in or separate meter before calculating exposure. This is automatic on most cartridge cameras. On a simple camera you cannot give different exposures so you must buy the correct film and shoot on a bright day.

Load the camera strictly according to the manufacturer's instructions. Cartridges: slot into camera back.

Roll film has a paper backing which must be threaded onto the take-up spool and wound on to the start of the film.

Cassettes: the leader is threaded onto the take-up spool and after 20 or 36 exposures the film must be wound back into the cassette.

The back of a 35mm camera opened to show the loading of a cassette film

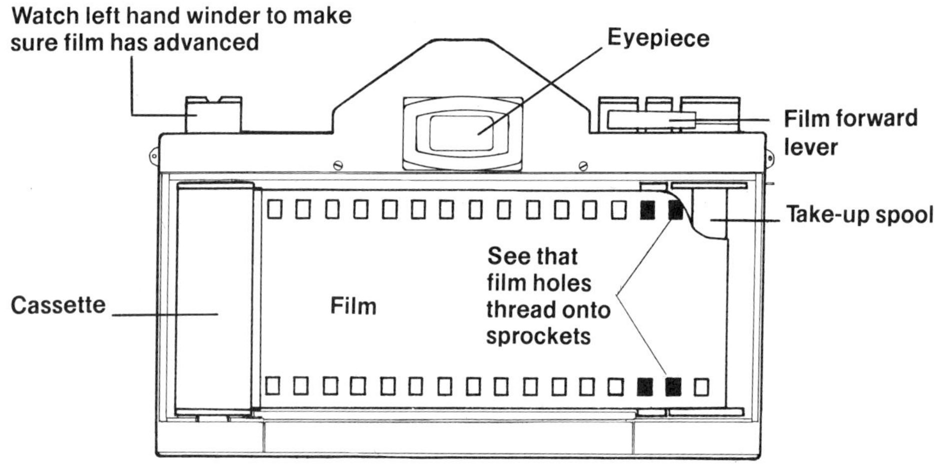

Calculate and set exposure

(This is the combination of shutter speed and aperture). You can use four basic methods for this:

a) Use the symbol settings on the camera.
b) Use the film manufacturer's chart (below).
c) Use an exposure meter.
d) Guess. (You need experience for this, but if all else fails try setting the camera at 1/125 at f11).

Dark subjects reflect less light and so they need relatively more exposure.

a) Symbol settings on simple cameras represent f/numbers. Select the symbol corresponding to the weather conditions.

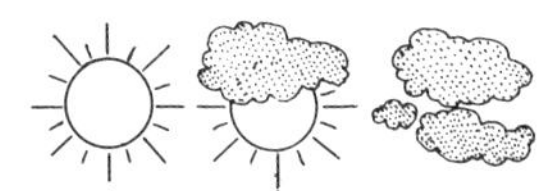

b) Use the film manufacturer's chart. These are packed with every film and are accurate for most subjects if used carefully. They are very good and thousands of dollars have been spent in the research for them. Don't throw them away; study them carefully.

c) Use an exposure meter. An exposure meter or light meter contains a light sensitive cell. This will measure the amount of light falling on or reflected off the subject and will translate this into a range of shutter speeds and f/numbers. You choose the combination you want.

Used properly, most exposure meters are very accurate. Really expensive ones are sensitive in extremely low light levels and can compute exposures of up to eight hours. Exposure meters are either built into the camera or are totally separate. There are also small meters that clip onto the top of a camera, sometimes coupling with the shutter speed or aperture setting. Some meters are powered by batteries that make them more sensitive. The batteries must be periodically replaced.

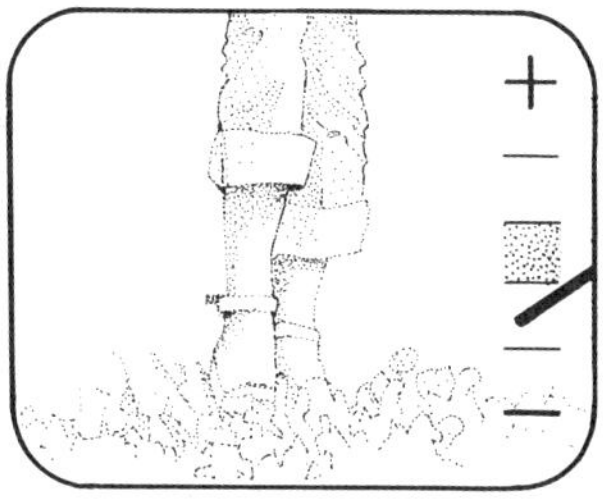

▲ *The viewfinder of a typical camera with built-in light meter.*

KODAK TRI-X PAN FILM
IN ROLLS AND 135 MAGAZINES

FILM SPEED ASA 400

DAYLIGHT EXPOSURE TABLE FOR *KODAK TRI-X* PAN FILM

Shutter Speed 1/500 Second	Shutter Speed 1/250 Second			
Bright or Hazy Sun on Light Sand or Snow	Bright or Hazy Sun (Distinct Shadows)	Cloudy Bright (No Shadows)	Heavy Overcast	Open Shade†
f/22	f/22*	f/11	f/8	f/8

*f/11 at 1/250 second for backlighted close-up subjects.
†Subject shaded from the sun but lighted by a large area of sky.

KODAK, TRI-X, HC-110, POLYDOL, MICRODOL-X, DK-50, KODAFIX, PHOTO-FLO, and D-76 are trademarks.

The exposure meter

Many modern cameras have built-in meters which are totally coupled to the shutter and f/number. To get the correct exposure the shutter speed or f/number is altered until the needle in the viewfinder reaches a certain point. These meters can be very accurate and some indicate the exposure being given in the viewfinder itself.

Separate exposure meters are versatile and very accurate. The light measurement taken with them is translated into a range of shutter speeds and f/numbers on a scale which is part of the meter. It is at this point that you must select the most suitable combination. Is it the shutter speed that is most important or the amount of the subject that is sharp?

Needle reading transferred to calculating scale

Film speed

f-number or aperture scale

Shutter speed scale

Back of meter

Light sensitive cell

Ways of using exposure meters

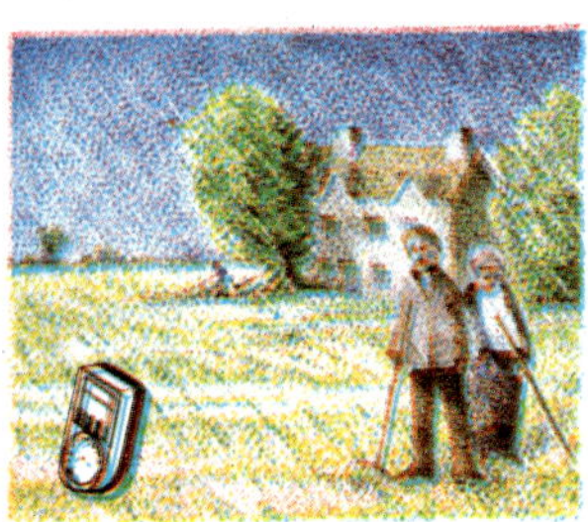

Integrated reading

This is a general reading of the light reflected off the whole subject and is good for normal subjects. (Do not include too much sky in the reading.) Built-in meters take this sort of reading.

Reflected light (close-up)

Take a reading off the most important part of your sub-

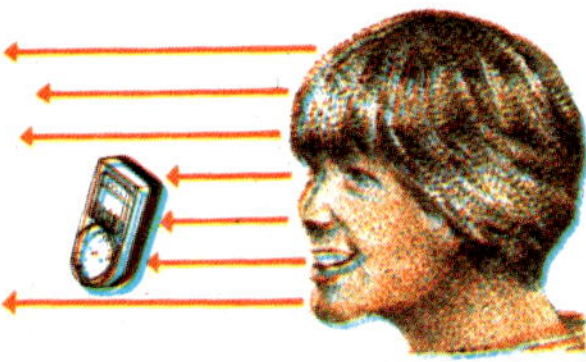

ject, e.g., face or person. Take it off an average tone, e.g., not a heavy shadow or bright highlight.

Incident light

Using a special attachment (usually a half-circle of white plastic), the light falling on the subject can be measured. Accurate method for use with color transparencies.

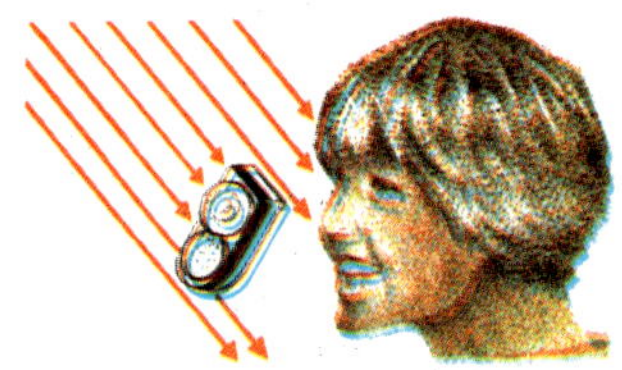

Hints on using exposure meters

a) If the subject is too far away to read off directly, read off a nearby equivalent, e.g., your own hand or a building. Take care that the tones are similar and that the lighting is the same.

b) When taking close-up readings do not let your shadow fall on the subject. This would alter the reading.

c) Do not include too much of the sky in the reading, as this influences the meter and gives a wrong (under-exposed) result. Keep the meter pointed slightly down. This is particularly true for built-in meters when photographing groups or landscapes. Try pointing the camera down slightly to take the reading, then reframe to expose. This may be impossible with automatics.

d) When shooting directly into the sun ("backlighting" or "against the light"), open up one stop on the indicated exposure if your camera allows this.

e) Color film, especially transparency material, needs to be exposed more accurately than monochrome.

f) Be careful when using automatic exposure single lens reflex cameras that light does not enter the viewfinder and upset the reading.

All these combinations give similar exposures

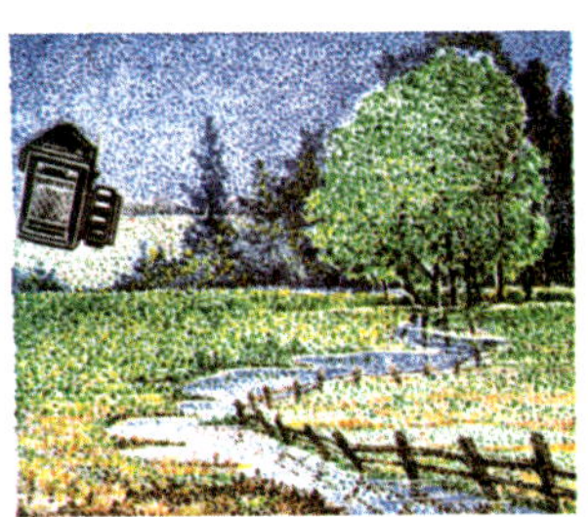

Sharpness		Average subject	Speed		
l/30	1/60	1/125	1/250	1/500	1/1000
f/16	f/11	f/8	f/5.6	f/4	f/2.8

For more depth of field (overall subject sharpness) choose these.

To stop moving subjects choose these combinations.

Judging your results

Once your prints or transparencies are processed you should check them to see if you are regularly over or underexposing. If you are, you can correct it in the future. Color prints are more difficult to judge than color transparencies, since automatic machines or printers compensate for exposure errors. If this has happened the prints will look rather flat and of poor quality. Overexposed pictures will have no highlight detail and underexposed pictures will be grayish with no shadow detail.

Errors of exposure in black and white can also be compensated for; overexposed pictures will look contrasty with no highlight detail and underexposed pictures will look gray with no details in the shadows.

Examples of exposures on transparencies.

▼ f/16 — one stop over ▼ f/11 — normal ▼ f/8 — one stop under

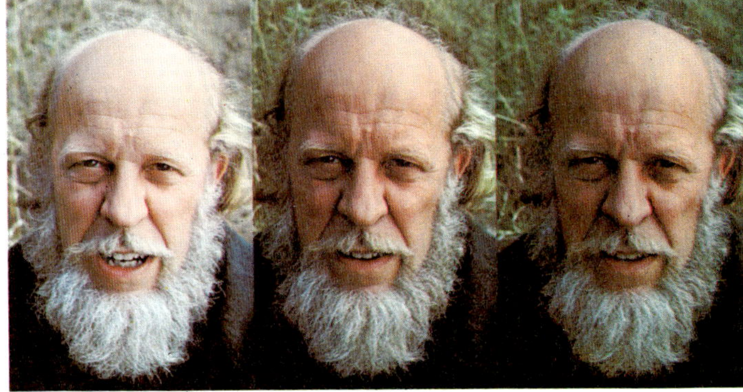

Effects of shutter speed and aperture

Moving subjects can be "frozen" by using a high shutter speed. The minimum speed needed depends on how close the subject is and the angle it is traveling at towards the camera.

Subjects moving parallel to the camera need a high shutter speed to stop movement, those traveling at 45° to the camera, a medium shutter speed, and those moving at 90° towards the camera, a relatively slow shutter speed.

Cameras with only slow shutter speeds can record movement from an angle or by shooting at the peak of action where motion has almost stopped.

The camera can also be "panned" at about l/60 second. Swing it keeping the subject in the center of the viewfinder. This will give a sharp subject and a blurred background.

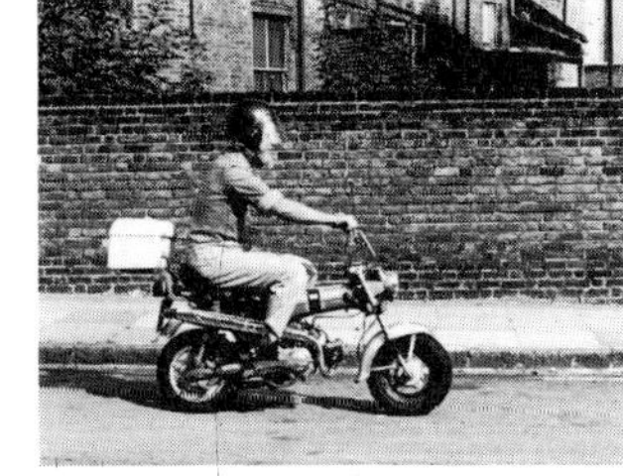

1

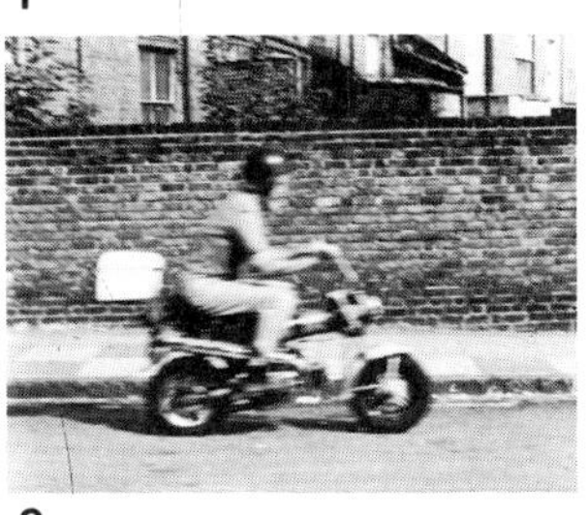

2

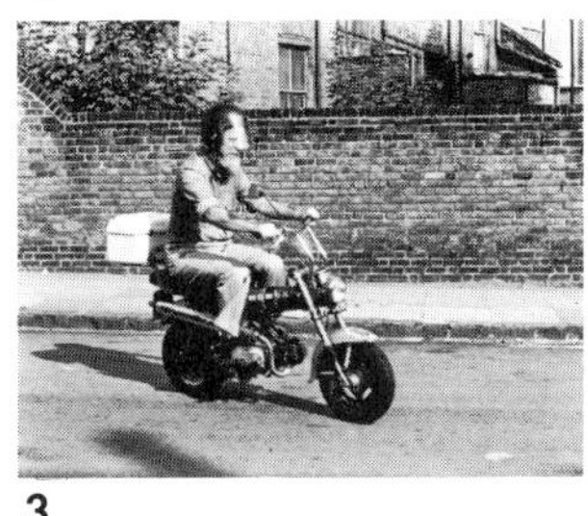

3

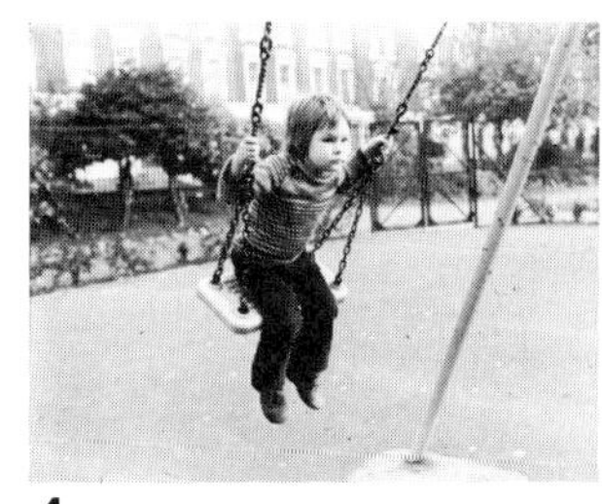

4

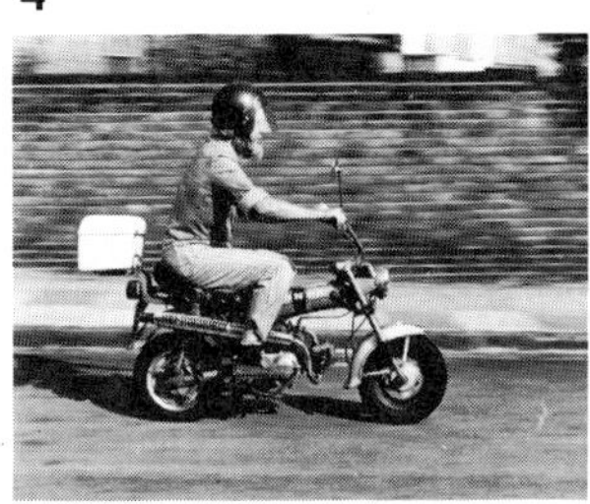

5

1. Fast shutter speed.
2. Slow shutter speed.
3. Angled subject.
4. Peak of action.
5. Panning.

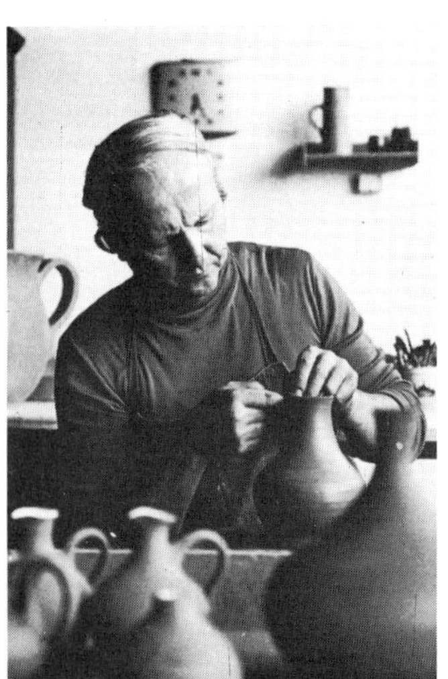

◀ *Large aperture – only part of the subject sharp. Background and foreground out of focus.*

▶ *Small aperture – greatest depth of subject sharp, including background and foreground.*

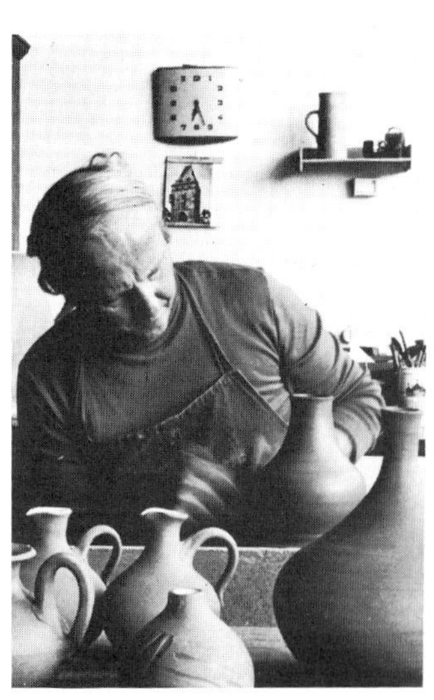

Focusing

All but the most simple cameras have some way of focusing. A box camera is permanently focused on 4 m. This means that at its fixed aperture of f/11 everything from 3 m. to infinity is sharp. There are various ways of calculating distances and setting focus.

a) Guessing or estimating.

b) Symbol settings on the camera.

c) With a tape measure or rangefinder.

d) With a focusing system built into the camera.

a) Set your estimate on the focusing scale of your camera. Imagine lying on the ground and you can estimate your height.

b) Use the symbol settings if your lens has them. They correspond to actual distances, e.g., a group represents 4 meters.

Close-up

Group (middle distance)

Distant scenes

c) Tape measures or separate rangefinders are good for extreme close up but measure from the back of the camera and not the front of the lens. Set the measurement onto the focusing scale on your camera.

d) More expensive cameras have built-in focusing. When you look through the viewfinder and turn the focusing ring on the lens you can see the image or rangefinder line markings go in or out of focus. You do not have to set

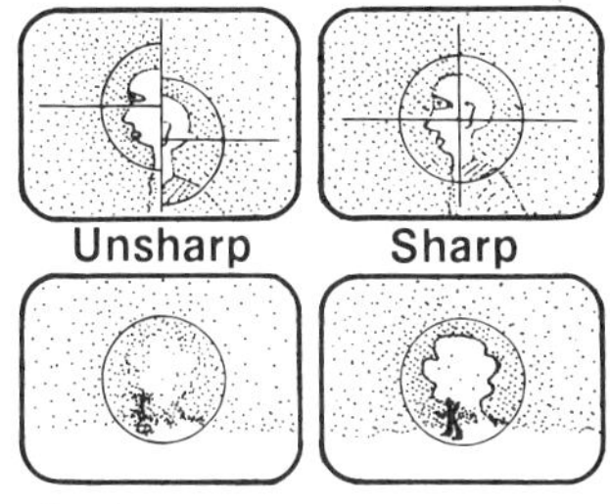

the focusing scale separately.

There are different kinds of built-in focusing systems but many are based on a circle in the center of the viewfinder.

Focusing hints

1. You need to focus more accurately for close-ups.
2. Remember that greater depth of field will give you more room for error when focusing.
3. If you don't want to draw attention to yourself and disturb a subject, first prefocus on something different but the same distance away.
4. If you want to photograph a fast-moving subject focus on a fixed point and press the shutter when the subject passes that point.
5. In low level lighting try to focus on something bright like a light bulb or a glowing cigarette. Wide-angle lenses are particularly difficult to use in these conditions.

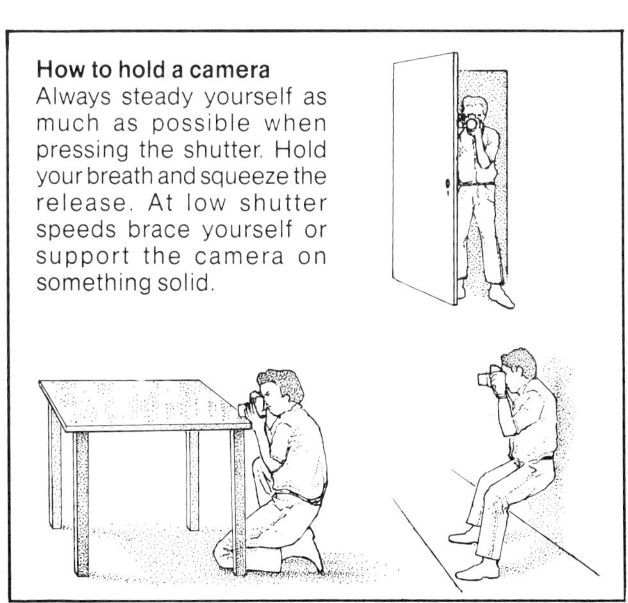

How to hold a camera

Always steady yourself as much as possible when pressing the shutter. Hold your breath and squeeze the release. At low shutter speeds brace yourself or support the camera on something solid.

Ways of Emphasis

We can look at what we please: whatever we look at, we look selectively. Other objects in our field of vision are rather blurred. But the camera records everything in its path with impartiality, regardless of its meaning or importance. This is one reason why so many technically perfect pictures are disappointing. In this section there are some ideas to help solve this problem. Every decision you make, of where, when, how, and whether to shoot depends on your answer to the question, "What do I want to show, and who is it for?"

Once this question has been answered, it is largely a matter of common sense as to how to emphasize what you want to show, and cut out or de-emphasize what is not necessary. In studio photography one has total control, but when you are photographing people you may not wish (or be able) to give instructions. Instead you can use the choice of viewpoint (where you shoot from) and timing (when you shoot) to control the lighting and the juxtaposition of subject matter. These are your tools for emphasis.

For example, if you are taking a picture indoors by the light from a window, the lighting on your subject will be different if you shoot from a different position. The juxtaposition of subject-matter will be affected both by your viewpoint and by your timing.

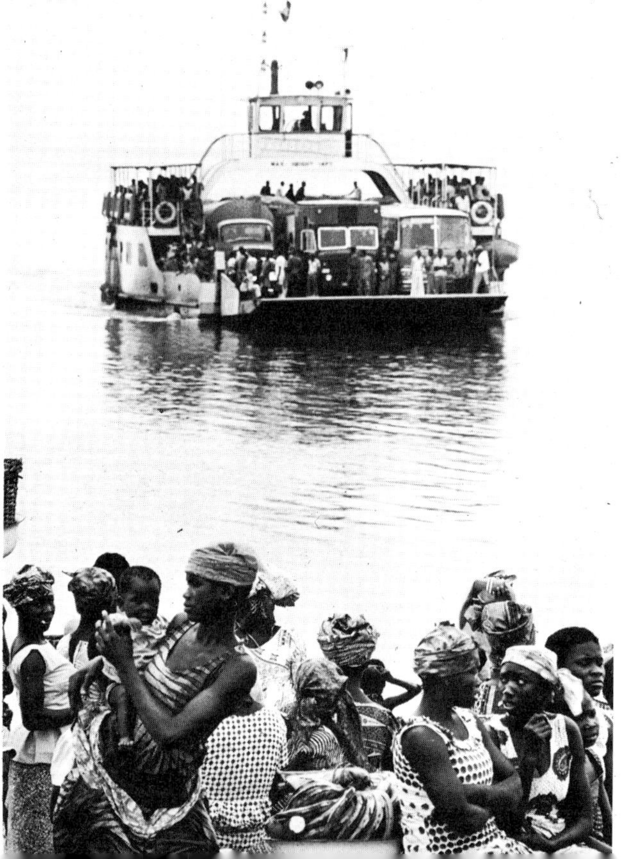

◀ *In this case viewpoint was used by the photographer to control juxtaposition of subject matter (a high angle separated background from foreground) but not lighting. Timing was also used to control juxtaposition (she waited till someone's face stood out clearly) but not lighting. The lighting was accepted as it existed – it was not very important in this photograph.*

Lighting, in terms of the way in which it gives character to and information about a subject, is dealt with on page 58. But first of all it is worth thinking of as a means of emphasis, by the way it picks out one part of the picture or another, giving or taking away emphasis and clarity.

In this respect there is no major difference between, say, a person who stands out in a picture by virtue of catching the light, or who stands out because he or she is wearing a white shirt. By waiting for, or creating, a juxtaposition of light against dark or vice versa, the part of the picture that you want to show can be made to stand out.

You have to make sure that the part which does stand out is the part which you do, in fact, want to emphasize. This is a skill which has to be learned by practice. One way to find out what does actually stand out visually in a subject is to screw your eyes up until you can barely see out of them. Notice how the shadows and dark areas lose detail, how shadows become more important, how objects you hadn't noticed in the background impinge on the main subject, and how subjects against a similar tone of background seem to disappear, while those against a contrasting background become dominant. At the same time, keep in mind the question "Who is it for?" and imagine them looking at your picture eyes half-closed. Does it show what you want it to show, loud and clear? If not, then you have either to move until your viewpoint makes it show (by virtue of the lighting or juxtaposition) or wait until there is some change which brings it about (timing).

There are many other ways of making your main subject stand out; for example, the background can be a contrast in texture (rough against smooth, etc.) or in pattern.

To some extent the camera can be used to separate the subject from its background, by the use of panning or differential focus. If the subject

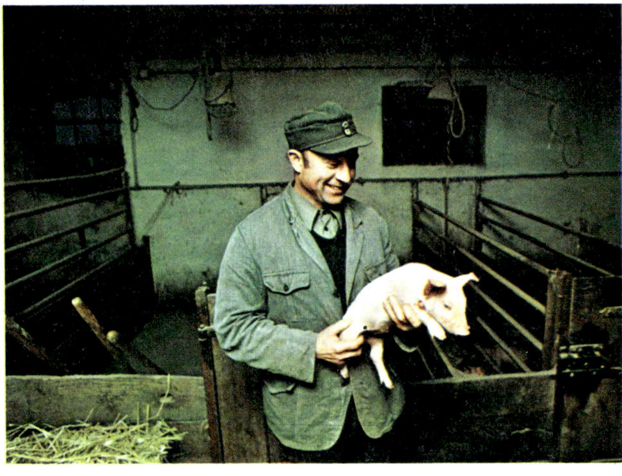

▲ *The lightest part of the picture stands out clearly.*

▼ *The light wall emphasizes the darker figure in front.*

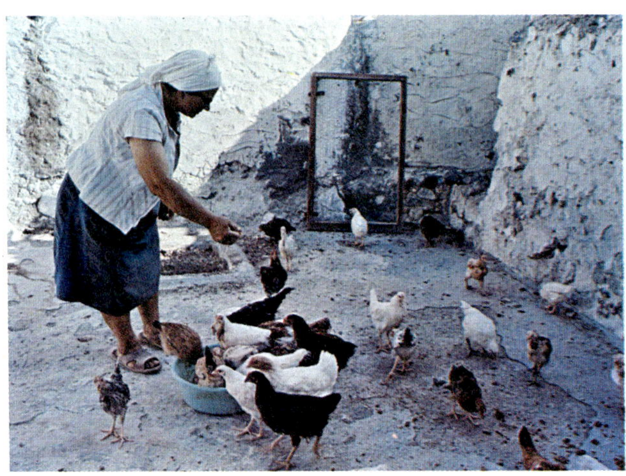

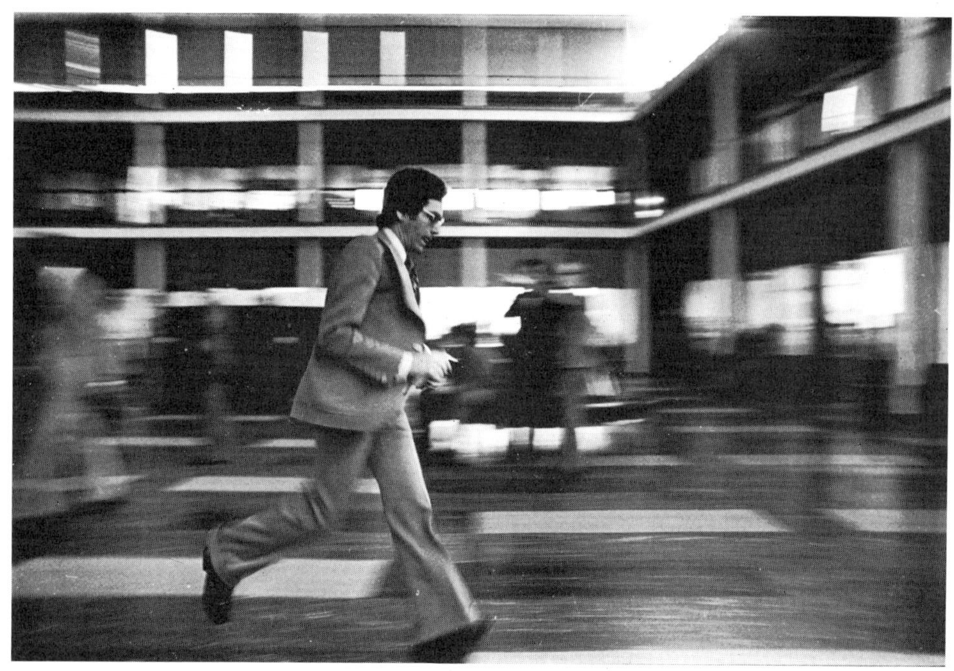

▲ *Panning with a slow shutter speed (1/15 sec.). Here the technique has been used to emphasize a specific aspect of the situation. This picture shows a jobber at Dusseldorf Stock Exchange running to buy stock at an advantageous price.*

is moving, you can follow it with the camera (see above) and blur the background. Differential focus is a method of keeping the background out of focus by using a large aperture (see p.29). However, unless you are using a long focus (telephoto) lens, or are very close to your subject, it is difficult to get it substantially blurred.

If you make a habit of squinting your eyes occasionally, you will notice other forms which tend to stand out, and build up an awareness of them: a sort of visual vocabulary. Edges, straight lines, curvy lines, squares, circles, and rectangles; trees and telegraph poles; cars, toys, electric cables, plugs, door-handles, fences, footpaths, litter... Where these have forms or meanings which do not help you to show what you want to show, you may have to find a viewpoint which loses them. But a strong line, frame, or half-frame can emphasize your subject powerfully.

It is often said that every picture must have one "center of interest." This is not always true. It depends on what you want to show and to whom. Of course, if you only want to show one thing, or if you know that your intended audience is not basically interested in your subject, then you do need a single point of emphasis. Advertisers often make their product the only point of emphasis, partly to make sure you look at it, partly because a single-emphasis picture is quicker to "read" and therefore has high impact.

But many good pictures have two or more points of equal emphasis (a picture of a football team might have eleven).

When you choose to have more than one point of emphasis, you are showing something more than just the person, or individuals, that you are photographing; you are showing something about relationships.

Pictures like this are often more interesting, but they do require more work on the part of the viewer than the "high impact" type of picture. People will generally only take the trouble to "read" a complex picture if they have some reason for doing so. They must either know the subject, or the subject must be so interesting that they want to have a good look anyway.

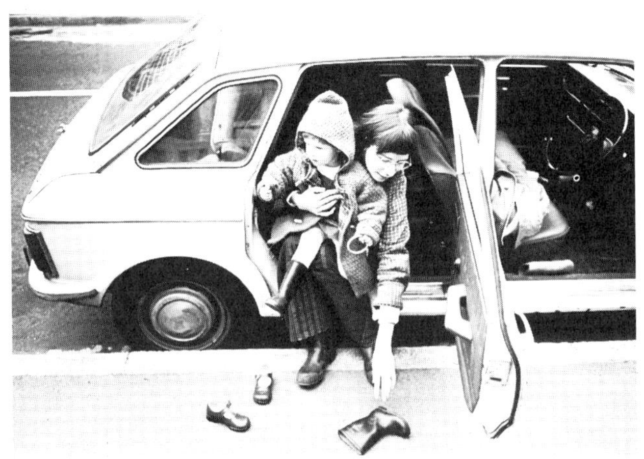

◀ *A line or edge accentuates whatever it encloses.*

▼ *The picture below, from a project to document the photographer's own life, is about class relationships. Look at it carefully. Does it support the previous explanation of emphasis? The three diners have one relationship with each other, a separate one with the waiters.*

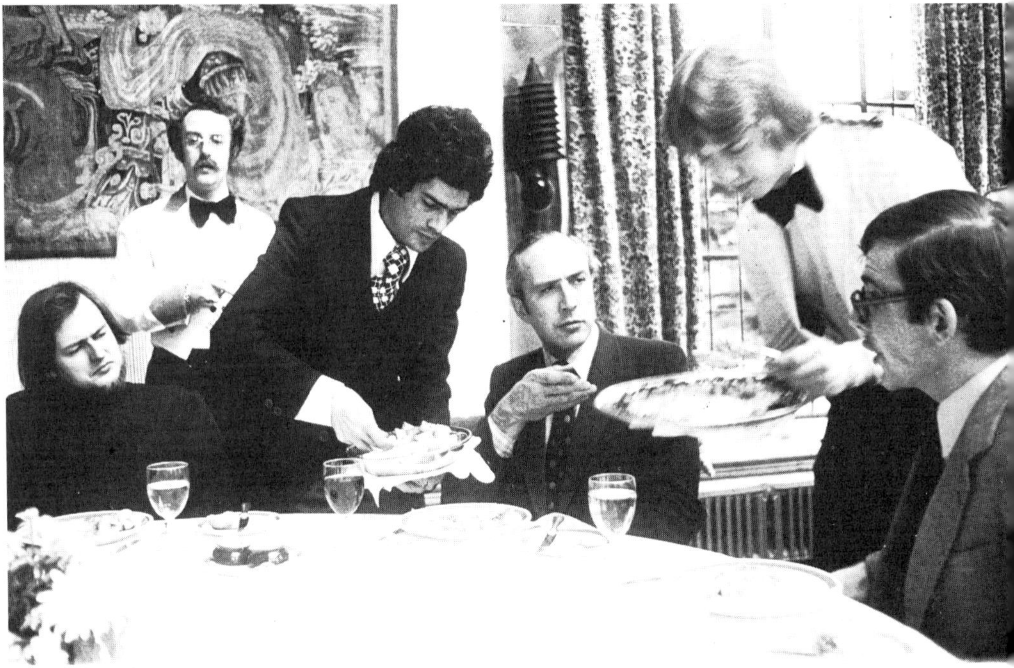

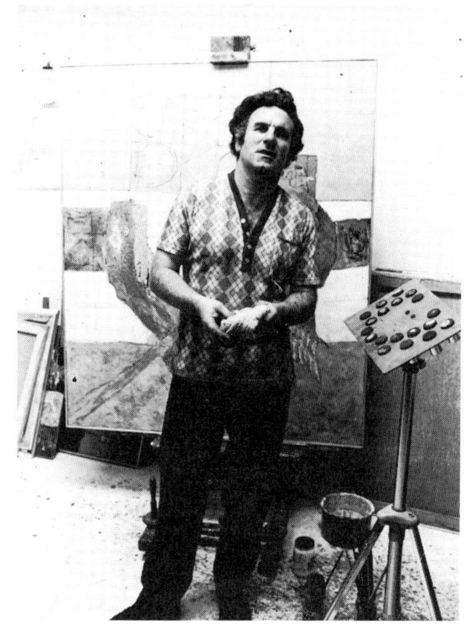

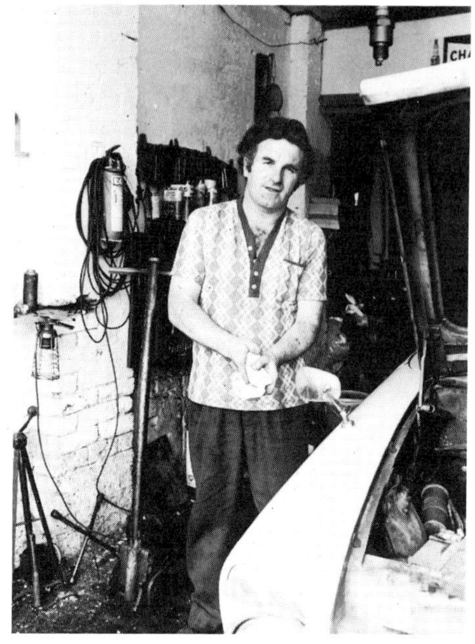

▲ *Changing the background changes the personality, which takes on the characteristics of the setting. Which is he, painter or mechanic?*

Supporting the main theme

As well as showing your subject clearly, you can also stress its qualities by association. (You can also imply qualities that are simply not there – some advertising does this.) If two subjects are in the same picture, there is an assumed relationship between them. Objects are assumed to belong to people near them. The known qualities of objects are attributed to people near them. Elements in a picture affect each other: qualities of one "rub off" on another. So if you want to emphasize particular qualities about your subject, it helps to include in the picture other elements known and agreed to have that sort of quality.

Another way of supporting the main theme is by contrast, which is much more tricky and may backfire. The main subject is placed in a setting of opposing meaning or quality. For instance, a beautiful girl in a beautiful dress is photographed in squalid surroundings, say in the poorest part of a city. Apart from the danger of "association" taking place, this is often considered to be in bad taste, as it can make people uncomfortably aware of the difference in lifestyles and living standards.

Another method of supporting the main theme by association is to use the tones, shapes, or colors of the picture evocatively: if they remind the viewer, however vaguely, of something, then the subject of the picture takes on some of those characteristics. For example, many important and dramatic news pictures are grainy and unsharp, so that these qualities have become associated with drama. Newspapers have occasionally made use of this to lend extra effect to a picture by using very fast film to copy and recopy a picture. Thus they deliberately degrade its quality and are able to imply, subtly, that the event photographed was more dramatic than it would have appeared if the picture had been of perfect quality.

In the same way, advertisers who wish to imply that their products have "good quality" require their photographers to use large format cameras, exquisite props, and a high standard of craftsmanship, so that the general feel of "quality" is associated with them.

These descriptions of emphasis methods are not exhaustive: they are merely guidelines toward a self-taught technique that can enable anyone to show what they want to show to the particular person or group of people that they have in mind. They do not deny the supremacy of content. Meaningful elements will have importance in a picture (faces will stand out, given the chance) but they will be helped or hindered by the visual technique.

However, many camera enthusiasts make the mistake of wanting to take nice pictures, which lack purpose. These can be rather pretentious and of little real interest.

▼ *In this advertisement in a medical publication for a skin-fold-dermatitis cream, props and lighting were used to create the image of an honest, slightly old-fashioned doctor, a lover of beautiful things (a sort of Dr. Welby). If he uses Timodine, it must be all right.*

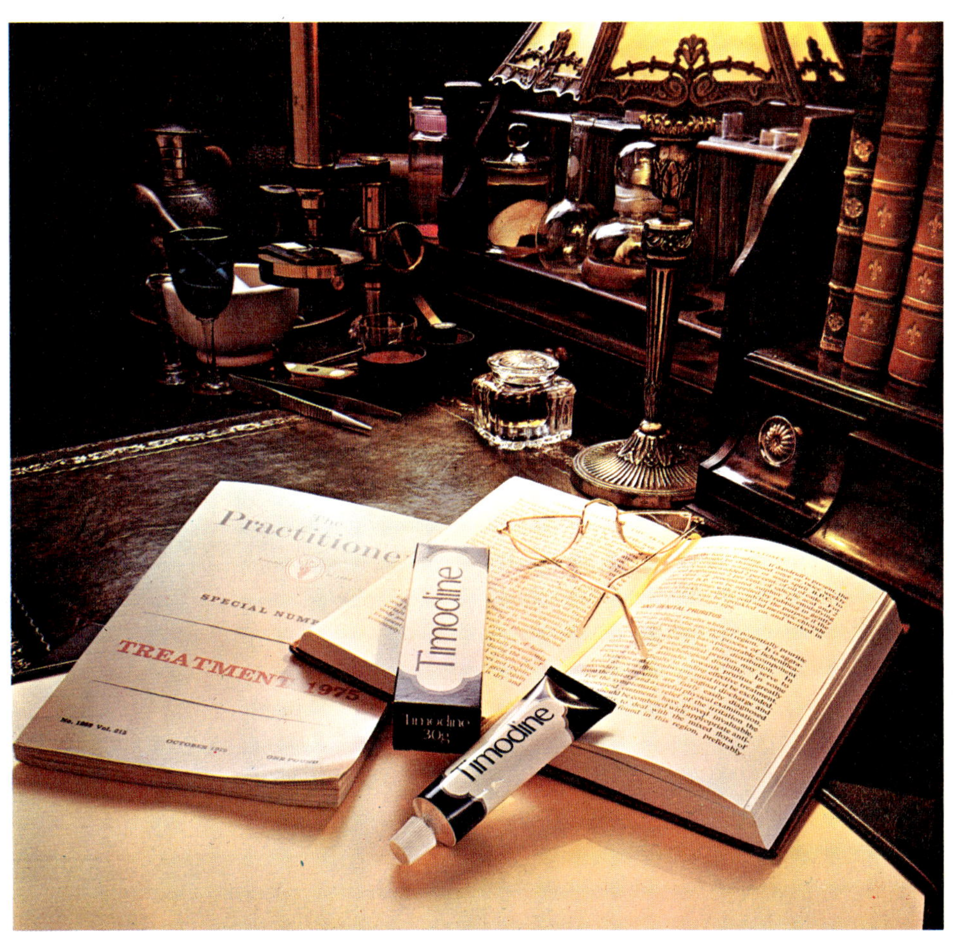

Understanding light

Lighting is one of the main factors in the success or failure of any picture, whether a studio still life, a landscape, portrait, family snapshot, or even (but to a lesser extent) a photojournalistic photograph. In still life work you can control the lighting completely, while photojournalists can only use their understanding of lighting to help them choose when and where to shoot. But the way that light behaves is the same in any situation. Good lighting is lighting that shows what you want to show (which usually means that it gives as much detailed information about your subject as possible) while at the same time conveying the "mood" that will reinforce it.

Of course, the most important function of light is simply to allow an exposure to be made. And if part of the picture isn't getting enough light, it will come out black. In most cases you need to have light falling on the main subject. If it does not (e.g., the face is in shadow) you may have to move the subject, change your own position, or wait until the lighting changes. In bright sunlight people's eyes sometimes look like black holes in their faces. For this reason many photographers try to avoid working in the middle of the day.

Good lighting is easy, and the easiest way to understand it is by doing a little studio lighting for yourself. You don't need expensive equipment; just a philosophy of simplicity:

OUT are spotlights, floodlights, baffles, booms, umbrellas.

OUT are "main light," "fill-in light," "hair light," "rim light."

OUT are hot spots and crossed shadows.

OUT is tripping over cables and sweating under the arc-lamps.

OUT is muddle, confusion, and mystery.

IN are a pair of scissors, some tracing paper, white and black paper or cloth, some silver foil, and a lamp (reflector and stand).

Basically your light can be anything, but it is easier if it is fairly powerful, such as a 200 watt household lamp or a photoflood (275 or 500 watt).

If you are using color transparency film it should be "tungsten" film, such as Type A or Type B (check instruction sheet). If you want to use flash, "daylight" color film is necessary.

You use the light on the stand as a starting point, or basic supply of light. It is like the sun. Then you can diffuse the light with tracing paper – as clouds diffuse the sun. You use the white or silver paper as reflectors – they are the equivalent of light colored walls or surfaces outside. The black paper or card, or the cloth, is to cut off the light, to stop it from falling where it is unwanted. This is the equivalent of anything outdoors that casts a shadow.

Now you have a controllable model lighting world. You can make the light do anything you wish.

You can recreate lighting conditions which are particularly effective in real situations, for example: the soft light on a misty morning, at dawn or sunset, indoors near a large window, in the shady part of a courtyard flooded with light, or indoors at night near a table lamp. If you can analyze the light that gives this effect naturally then you can reproduce it artificially. And if you can't produce it artificially, then you will at least be able to look for it occurring naturally.

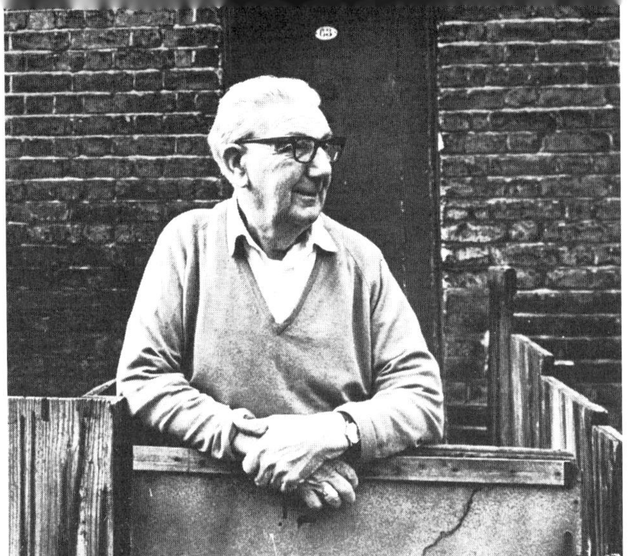

▲ *Large-source lighting from an overcast sky. Similar to . . .*

▼ *Large-source lighting from flash bounced off the ceiling.*

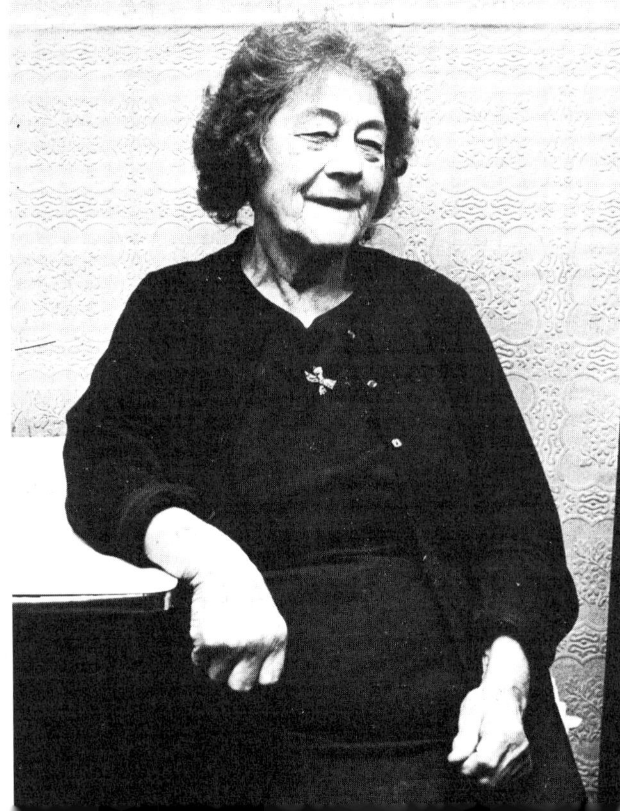

How to analyze lighting

Various words are used to describe light: hard, soft, direct, bounced, flat, back lighting, and so on. Different people mean different things by them, so the terms are not reliable tools for analyzing light. A better method is to break lighting down into five variables, of which the most important seems to be:

1. The size of the light source. (The word *source* is used here to mean whatever actually illuminates the subject, i.e., the reflector or diffuser rather than the light bulb,etc.) **A large light source** gives lighting that is almost nondirectional, with barely visible shadows, very gradual modeling, and very large highlights that would only be visible on a very shiny surface. Large-source lighting occurs on an overcast or foggy day, where the direct sunlight is cut off by a thick cloud, building, etc., so that the sky becomes the main source. When you bounce a flash off the ceiling, the ceiling becomes a large light source.

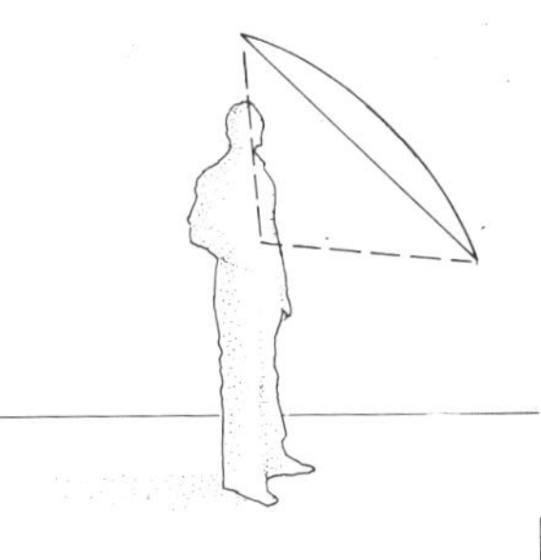

Large light source

You can create a large light source in the studio by bouncing light off the ceiling, or by using a large white reflector or diffuser quite close to the subject (i.e., so that the distance from reflector to subject is half, or less, the diameter of reflector).

A large light source shows the subject matter clearly but with little emphasis. It is usually undramatic, bland, or calm. It is useful for very complex pictures as it avoids the further complexity of shadows, and holds the picture together well. Colors stand out well in large-source lighting, even though they are not actually as saturated as with smaller source lighting. Examples: groups of people, group photographs.

A small light source, at the other extreme, gives highly directional light with pronounced, hard-edged shadows, harsh modeling with little feeling of roundness, and very small highlights (smaller on shiny objects, more spread out on matt ones). Small-source lighting occurs outdoors when the sun shines directly on the subject, when flash is used "direct," and in the studio when the studio light falls directly on the subject, or is bounced off a very small reflector some distance from the subject. (There is no inherent difference between "direct" and bounced light: the difference only occurs where the size of the source is different.)

Although the sun is 866,400 miles in diameter, it is still effectively a small light source! This is because it looks small (in area) to the subject. Conversely, a piece of white card only one meter across is a large light source if it is held very close to the subject. The quality of light given depends on the apparent size of the light source as far as the subject is concerned.

A small light source is the most difficult to handle well. It casts complicated shadows everywhere, often where they are not wanted, e.g., in the eyes or across faces. It doubles up the number of elements in the field of view, as each object gains a shadow. Small-source lighting is useful where you want to make a single or simple subject more complex. For example, if you

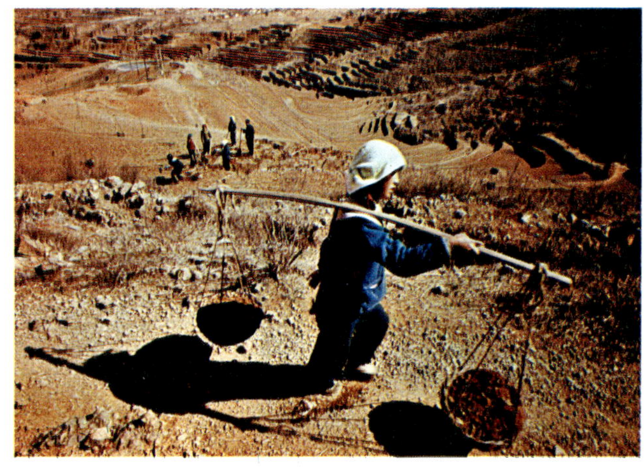

▲ *Small-source lighting (direct sunlight).*

▼ *Small-source lighting (direct flash).*

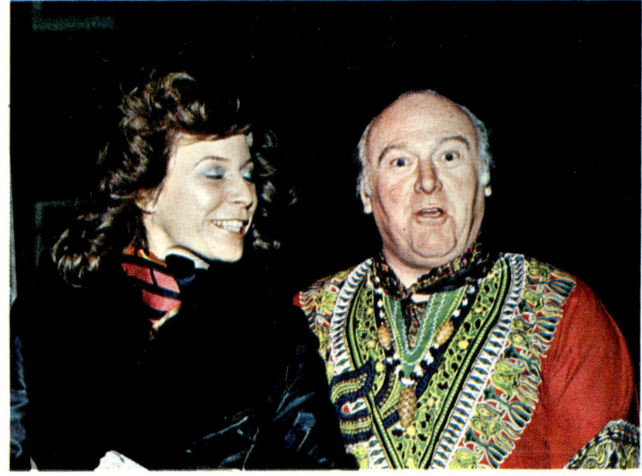

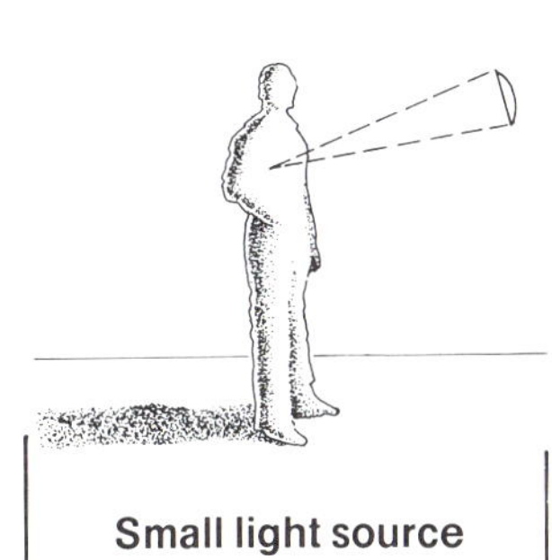

Small light source

want to show someone's face as heavily lined and furrowed, small-source light from the side will do this. Exactly the same effect will be produced on the surface of a building, especially with side light. So if you want to bring out extra texture on something, and the shadows are not a problem, use small-source lighting. (But note that a medium-sized source will also show texture if it is from the side, while at the same time giving better overall modeling for shape.)

A medium-sized light source gives lighting that is directional, with definite but soft-edged shadows, rounded and rich modeling, and definite but not overpowering highlights. On shiny objects such as bottles or cars the shape of the highlight can be used to bring out the shape of the subject. If you place a dark colored bottle near a window the

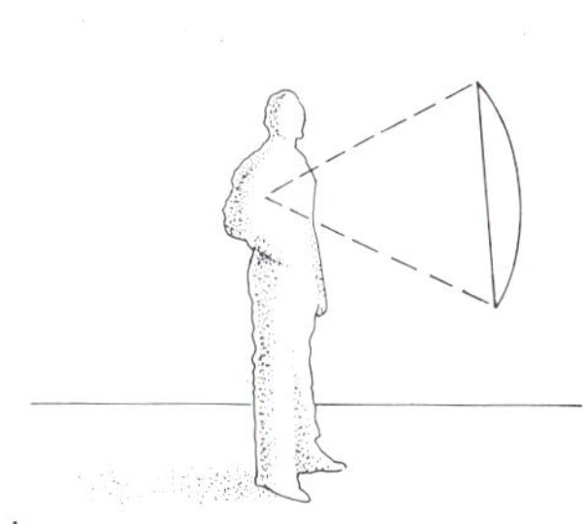

Medium-sized light source

highlight will run down the neck onto the body of the bottle, showing its shape much better than the pinpoint highlight produced by a small source.

Medium-source lighting occurs outdoors when the

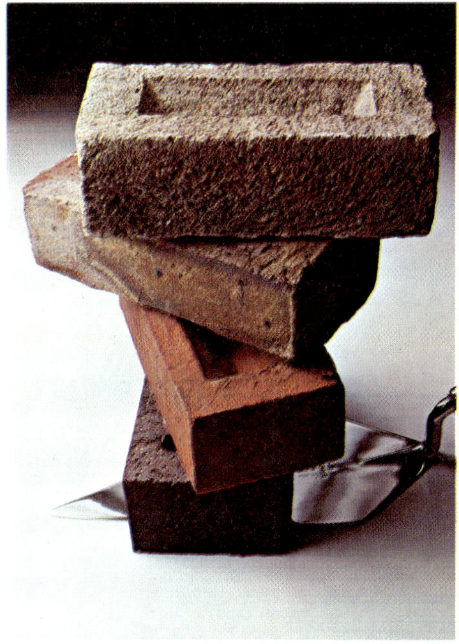

▲ *Medium-source lighting (flash and diffuser).*

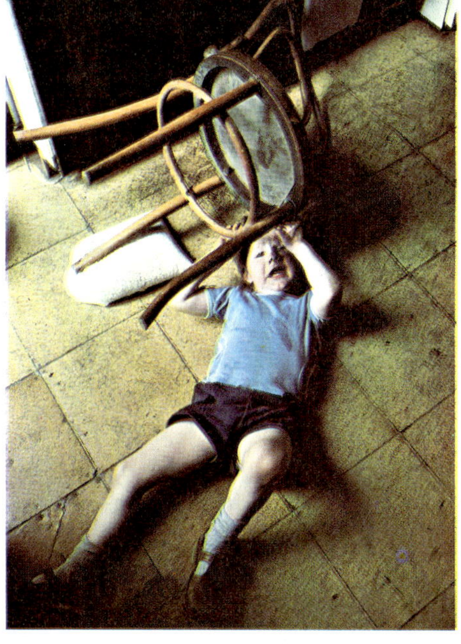

▲ *Medium-source lighting (window).*

sun strikes a wall or light-colored surface and this in turn lights the subject. It occurs indoors when the subject is near a window but not in the direct sun. It can be created in the studio by bouncing the light from a piece of white card, when the size of the card is roughly the same as its distance from the subject, or by placing a diffuser in a similar position and lighting through it. If you are using a flash you can create a medium-sized source by pointing the flash at a wall if the wall is quite close to the flash and the subject, for example, one meter and two meters, respectively.

Medium-source lighting is very beautiful and seductive. It gives a gentle gradation of tone all the way from highlight to shadow area, with some texture but not too much. Painters such as Vermeer used it. Still life photographers use it almost exclusively. You can vary the size to get more vigorous or more delicate lighting, making the source slightly smaller or larger. It can be used in almost any situation. For outdoor portraiture place your subject near a sunlit wall (but without direct sun on his or her face).

2. The position of the light source. That is, its angle to the subject.

Except with very small light sources, slight changes in the angle of the light do not have very much effect. Think rather in terms of basically different angles, such as front, back, top, side, or half-side.

Front lighting has a strange quality of "take-it-or-leave-it" punchiness. It is not "normal" or neutral except insofar as one has become used to it in flash photographs where the flash is mounted on the camera. However, it does reveal quite a lot of information in the subject. If the source is large it is not so noticeably "front lit."

Back lighting is for beauty, not for information. It is highly evocative of sunrises, sunsets, (cowboys riding into), soft music, and self-indulgence, and it's lovely. But if you have an interesting subject back lighting is likely to coat it in too much sugar.

Top lighting is theatrical (as is also lighting from below, of course) or very matter-of-fact, according to the size of the source and the lightness of the background. Still life photographers frequently use a medium source directly above the subject, with the

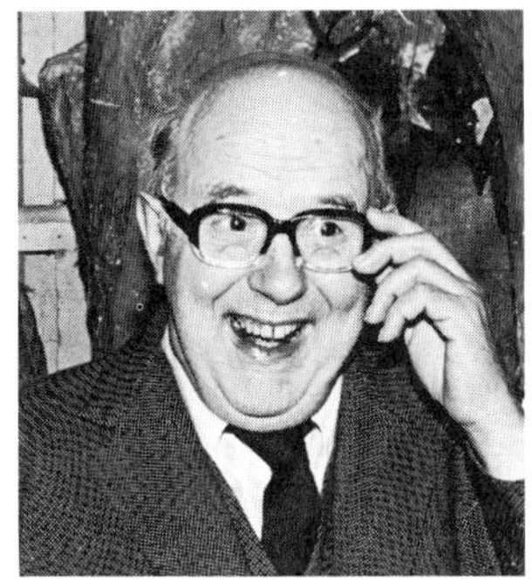

▲ *Front lighting (flash on camera).*

▼ *Back lighting (direct sunlight).*

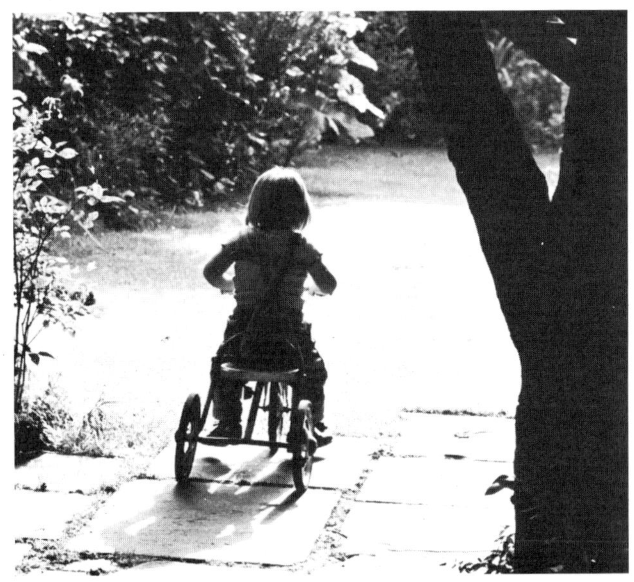

light falling away into blackness in the distance. On the other hand, large source top lighting on an overcast day is about as undramatic as they come.

Side lighting is especially useful for showing texture, and is therefore very important in architectural photography.

Half-side lighting is what might be called "normal" lighting. It is clean and efficient, shows detail and information well, no fuss, no problems. If your subject is interesting, half-side lighting is a straightforward and honest way of presenting it.

Generally speaking, the further toward the back that your lighting is, the more dramatic it becomes, and vice versa. So if you can't control the size of your light source, you can make your lighting slightly more exciting by moving one way, or slightly more information-giving by moving the other.

3. The distance of the light source from the subject. If the source is very close to the subject, it lights it unevenly, which is evocative of firesides, table lamps, etc. — thus a feeling of coziness or intimacy is produced. A more distant source lights the subject evenly, coldly, cleanly.

4. Where the light falls. By cutting off the light from your background or main subject you can control the way in which the subject stands out, or create particular effects (see above). Use a black card or cloth for precise control in the studio; large light sources are not so controllable as medium and small ones.

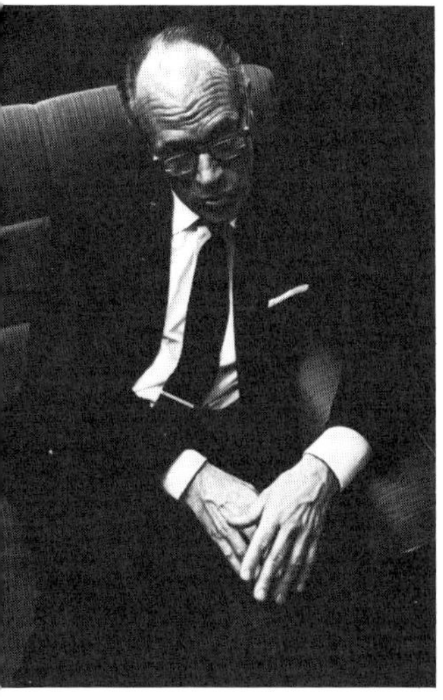

◀ *Top lighting (window).*

▼ *Side lighting (studio light direct -tungsten).*

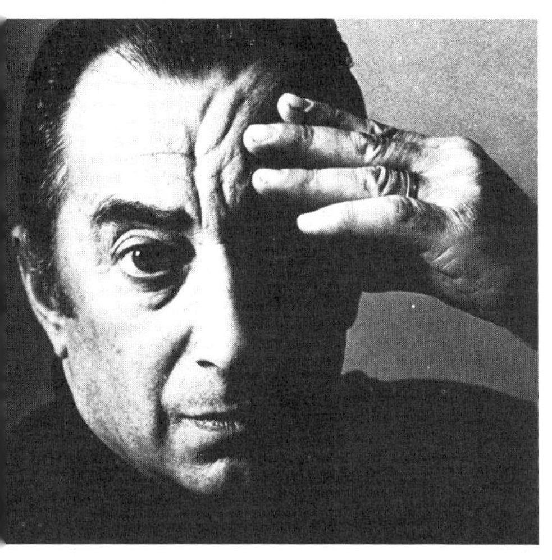

▼ *Half-side lighting (window).*

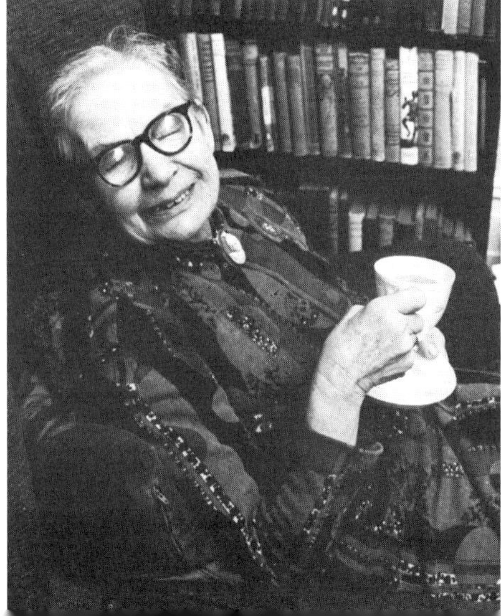

5. The amount of light in the shadows. If there is no light in the shadows they will appear black. By definition, no light from your main light source reaches them directly, so you may need to put some in. In the studio, one is tempted to plug in a second lamp – but the results can be disastrous. If you get any shadows from the second source, or any highlight or even any significant modeling, your original lighting will be destroyed. Your lighting of the shadows should reinforce the main lighting.

If shadow lighting is from a source smaller than the main light it will look artificial and "studio-ish." It is much safer to use reflectors to bounce some of the main light back into the shadows. Ideally the fill-in should just be on the same side of the camera as the main light; if it is opposite you will get subtle cross lighting. Shadows from the fill-in will run in the opposite direction to the main shadows (even if they are invisible!) and destroy the modeling.

Outdoors, the question of light in the shadows is vital. In direct sunlight (small-source lighting) they tend to go black, losing important information and breaking up the picture. If you are taking a portrait, a sheet of paper or even a newspaper solves the problem. Photojournalists sometimes wear a white shirt, dress, or sweater as a reflector. You may be able to work near a white or light-colored wall: or you may have to wait till the sun is slightly diffused by clouds. In the evening, the relative strength of the sun is weaker compared with the light reflected back from the ground, and a slight mist solves all your problems.

How much light you put into the shadows depends on whether you want to show important detail in them or whether you want the richer, more powerful effect of dark shadows. Screw up your eyes to judge how it will look to the camera. Choose the level of fill-in that is most evocative of the idea you wish to put across.

It all depends on what you want to show and whom you want to show it to.

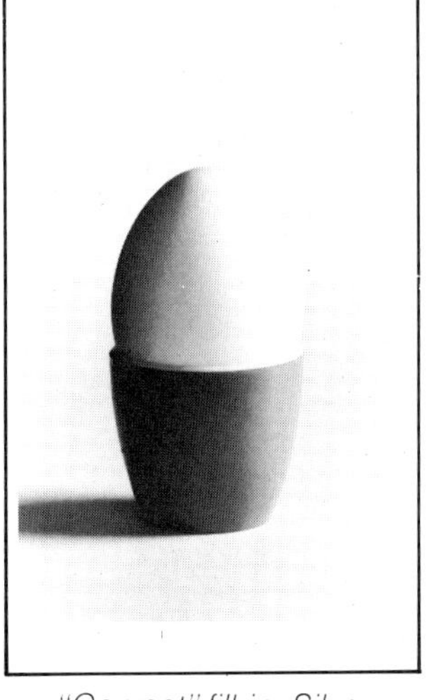

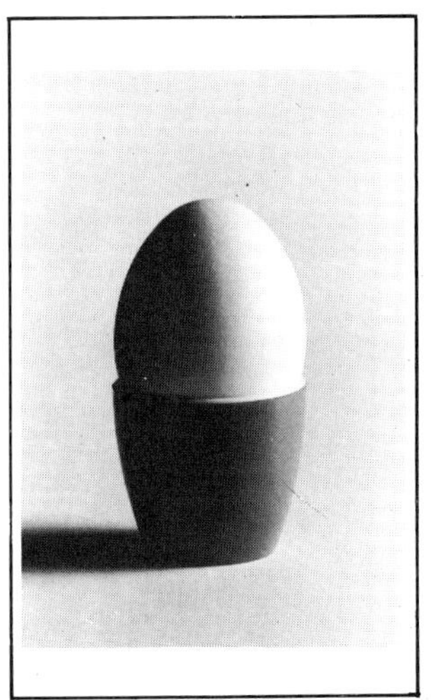

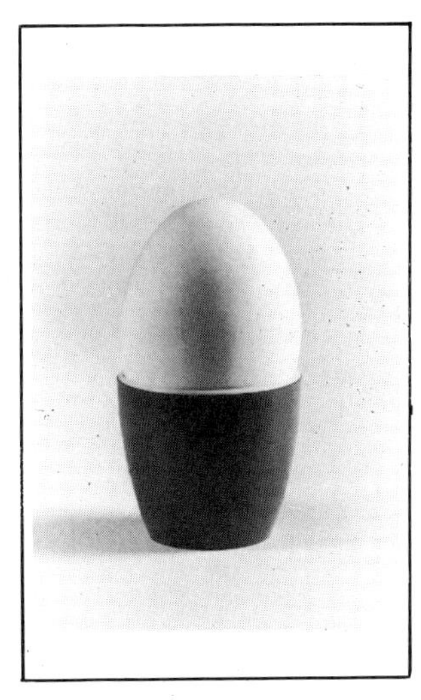

▲ *"Correct" fill-in. Silver reflector near camera, on same side as main light, adds to roundedness of egg. (If this is not practical, use a large white reflector as frontally as possible.)*

◀ *No fill-in (studio light through diffuser – tungsten).*

▶ *Wrong fill-in. Silver reflector opposite main light.*

When the lights are low

Photojournalists and press photographers often have to work in difficult lighting conditions – shooting indoors and when it is nearly dark. For them the first consideration is not necessarily "is the light beautiful?" but "is there enough light to make an exposure?"

In general you cannot hold a camera steady at a shutter speed of less than 1/30 sec. and very few lenses have a maximum aperture wider than f2 or f2.8.

If your meter or your chart indicates that you need more exposure than your camera allows for, you can do one of several things:

1. Use a faster film, say 400 ASA rather than 125 ASA. This will enable you to give shorter exposures. There are even faster films on the market.

2. Use a tripod (and a cable release). This will enable you to give long time exposures. Obviously it is not much use for photographing moving subjects like people unless you want special blurred effects, for example at ½ second. It could be good for room interiors or street scenes at night.

▼ *Street market in Bombay at night. Taken at 1/15 second with a hand-held camera steadied against a wall.*

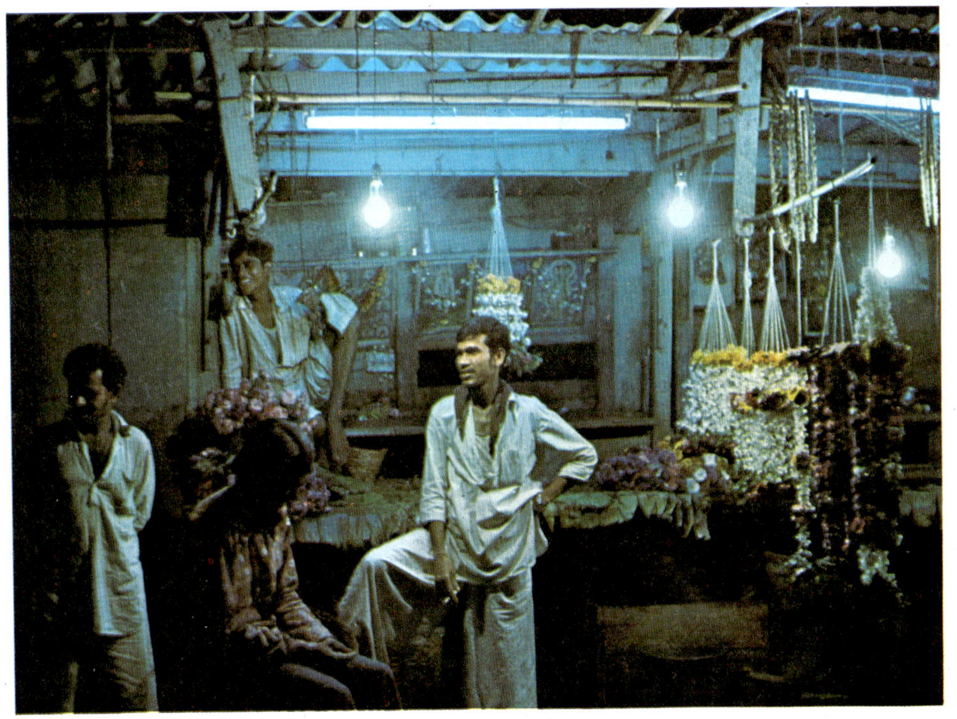

3. Steady yourself and the camera in some way so that you can give exposures of 1/10 – 1/2 second handheld. This is useful if you want to take pictures unobtrusively.

4. B/w only. Use a special developer to increase the apparent speed of your film. You can buy these in most photography shops. You can also do this by increasing development times – Tri X in D 76 diluted 1 + 1 for 15 mins. can be rated at ASA 800. But remember that in order to gain speed you will lose quality. The picture will be more "grainy" and fuzzy. Only use these methods if you have to.

Color: If you take color transparency films to a professional lab, you can ask them to uprate the film speed for you, but it costs more and changes the colors.

5. Use extra tungsten lighting. This should be matched for any color film you are using (consult manufacturer's leaflet). One way is simply to put up photoflood bulbs or tungsten halogen lights on stands and light the scene rather like a studio, either directly or by bouncing the lights off the ceiling as a TV crew would do. Needless to say this disturbs people and disrupts the event you are photographing and would often be impossible (for example, in a jazz club). Another method is to replace the existing light bulbs with brighter, shortlife photoflood bulbs. (Beware of melting the light fitting.) This raises the level of illumination without changing the nature of the lighting. People soon adapt to the brighter lights. This is a good method to use in people's houses or work places.

6. Use a bulb or electronic flash (see next section). As well as providing portable illumination, electronic flash enables high speed actions to be photographed, since a single flash is very short, (e.g., 1/1000 sec.).

▼ *Sunday night, Bentonia, Mississippi. Maximum use of available light.*

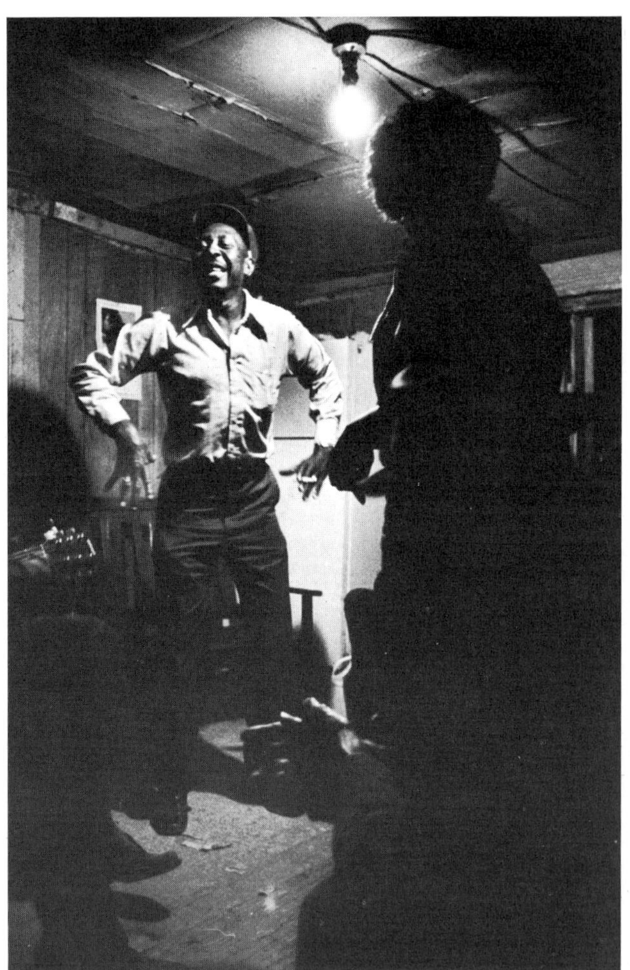

Flash

There are two basic kinds of flash: expendable bulbs (including cubes), and electronic. If you don't use the flash often, bulbs are cheaper.

All flash guns need linking to the camera through an electronic contact to synchronize the shutter and the flash. With most you must calculate which aperture to use. Easy charts help you do this and some electronic units are computerized. The aperture depends first on the power of the unit and the film speed (together these are given as a guide number) and second, on the distance from the flash to subject.

Flash only illuminates subjects up to about 20 feet away. It's no good trying to brighten up your sunset pictures by firing off a bulb at the 93,000,000 mile distant subject. The same goes for distant views and pictures from high buildings.

Bounced flash

A flash fired directly at the subject gives harsh lighting. Try bouncing it off a light wall or ceiling to give an effect similar to daylight. It is not possible to bounce computerized units unless they have been designed to do this.

With manual units, for an average room, open up two stops after your basic calculation and measure the total distance the flash travels. When using color, bounce off white only or everything in the photograph will turn out the color of the wall.

Check list

1. Attach unit to camera.
2. If necessary plug synchronization lead into camera. Bulbs – M synchron. Electronic – X synchron.
3. Set shutter speed. Diaphragm shutter – up to 1/500. Focal plane shutter – up to 1/30.
4. Calculate aperture.
5. Fire shutter when ready.

▲ *Direct flash is harsh.*

▼ *Bounced flash is softer but you have to open the lens two stops.*

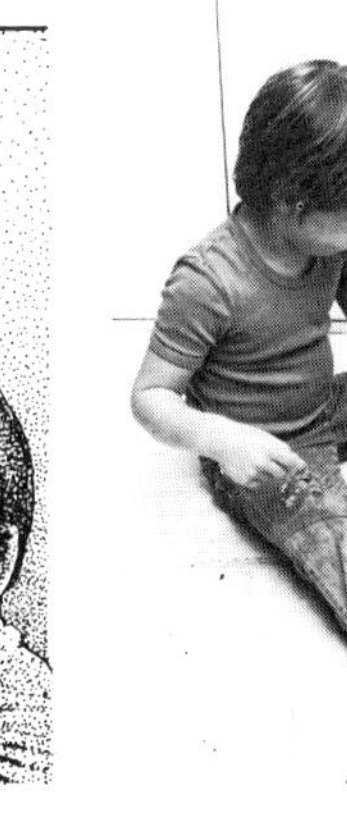

$$\frac{\text{guide number}}{\text{flash to subject distance}} = \text{aperture}$$

$$\text{example: } \frac{110}{10 \text{ feet}} = f/11$$

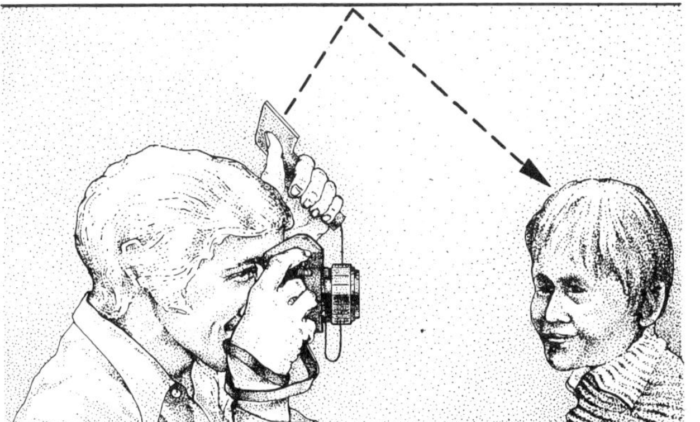

Darkroom work

When you have finished shooting a roll, cassette, or cartridge of black and white film, you can either take it to a photo processing center and have it developed only, then go straight to the next stage of making contact prints; or, if you want to be certain that your pictures will get the best possible treatment, do it yourself. As long as you keep to the following instructions and take your time, developing film is not difficult — anyone can do it.

YOU WILL NEED

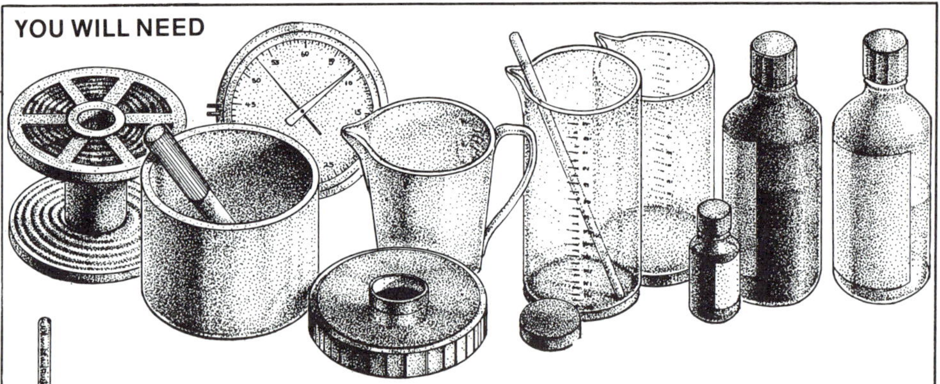

Equipment

1. Developing Tank
   The plastic autoload type is by far the easiest to load. (Stainless steel tanks are more durable but require more skill.) Secondhand tanks tend to stick.
2. A measuring cup or bottle
3. Two other jugs or beakers
4. A stirring rod (plastic or glass)
5. A clock (or watch with second hand)
6. Two bottles to store developer and fixer for further use. The developer bottle should be dark-colored and have an air-tight cap. Label bottles clearly.
7. A thermometer covering 15 – 30°C (60 – 90°F).
   Household utensils are fine for most of the above.
8. (If possible) a friend who has done it before.

Materials

1. Developer and fixer suitable for film. The developer should be bought in fairly small quantities as it does not keep well. Powder form is cheaper but liquid form chemicals are easier and quicker to mix up.
2. Wetting agent in a small bottle.

Warning
Electricity and water can make a lethal combination, especially for children. Don't touch the light switch with wet hands. Keep cables, etc., away from the "wet area."

SETTING UP

The first stage of developing film – breaking open the roll, cassette, or cartridge and loading the developing tank MUST BE CARRIED OUT IN TOTAL DARKNESS, or the film will be "fogged," that is, it will go black or gray all over.

Suggestions

If you don't have a darkroom you could:

1. Do the loading in someone else's darkroom and take the tank home to do the developing later.
2. Load at night under several thick blankets (hot, sticky, and

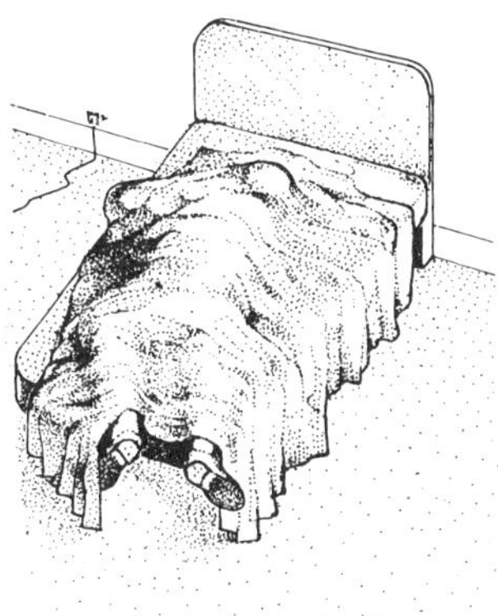

not much fun...). As you struggle under the blankets remember that sweaty thumbprints cannot be removed from the emulsion side.

3. Use a commercial loading bag (expensive and just as hot and sticky).
4. Buy a daylight-loading tank: expensive/unreliable.
5. Use a wardrobe or closet, preferably at night (cheap and reliable but... check that the

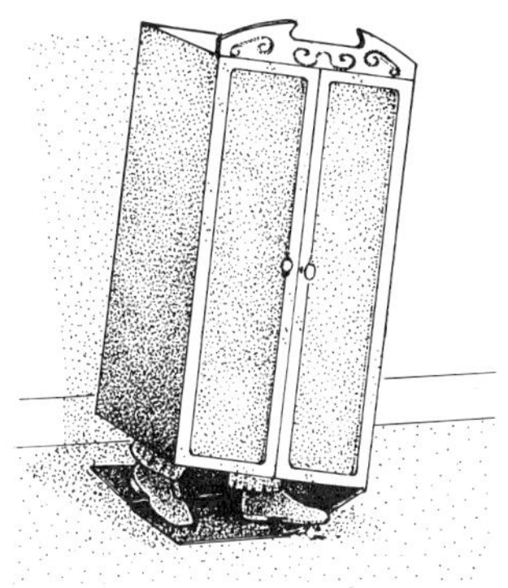

floor of the wardrobe is strong).

6. Set up a proper darkroom. You need to completely black out any windows. Try black polyethylene, or several coats of black paint. The darkroom needs a dry area (such as a table, for loading) and a sink or wet area for processing, preferably with hot water available. (Of course, the sink can be in a different room.)

Loading the spiral is the most tricky part of the operation; the rest is easy. If you can get someone to show you how to do it, it is much easier. Practice loading in daylight using old film. When you can do it easily, practice loading with your eyes shut. Then practice in the dark.

Procedure

Place tank, lid, and spiral on a clean, dry, flat surface and note their positions. Hold the film ready to open.

White light off

Cartridge (110): Break open cartridge. Remove film. Cassette (35 mm): Pull off the end of the cassette and take out the film. Cut off the leader. (The part you see when you load the camera, with perforations one side only.)

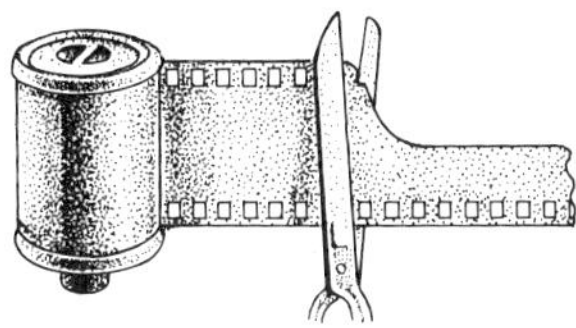

Roll Film (120): Break seal, unroll, and separate film from backing paper.

Feed the film into the spiral as far as it will go. It is the right way around if the natural curl of the film goes the same way as the curve of the spiral. Handle only by the

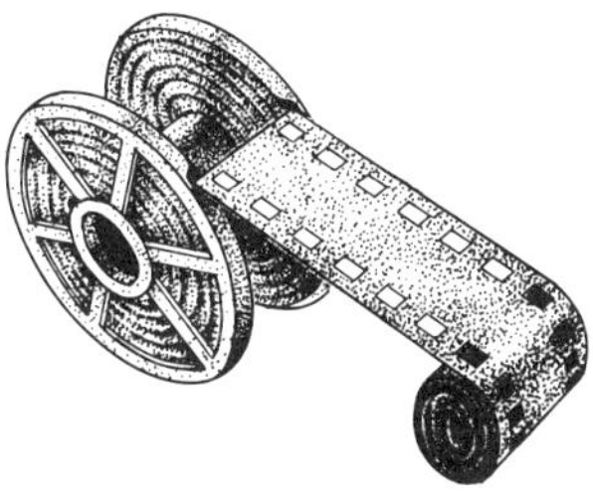

edges. When the film has gone in as far as it will, change your grip. Turn alternate sides of the spiral, until the film is all wound on. If it jams, shake it, but never force it. If all else fails, put everything in a bowl of water and load underwater. (Keep the film in water in the tank until you are ready to process.) Put the spiral in the tank right way up, and replace the lid.

White light on 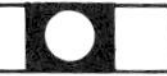

MIXING THINGS

Mix fixer first, using measuring cup or bottle, according to manufacturer's instructions. Store in a bottle marked clearly "fixer." Wash everything out very carefully after it has been in contact with fixer.
Remember...

> **Fix'll fix it**
> Small traces of fixer will ruin your film and prints, contaminate the developer, and stain or bleach clothes. Always rinse after using fixer. Keep it off your towel and taps.

1. When developer is at 20°C pour into tank and start the clock (or check watch).

2. Tap the tank on the bench to free air bubbles and agitate for 10 sec. by twisting the knob or inverting. Make sure the cap is on.

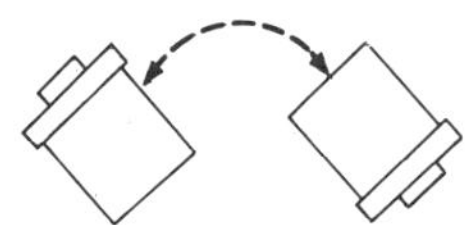

8. Take film out of spiral. Run your (clean) fingers down it to remove excess moisture and hang it up to dry away from dust.

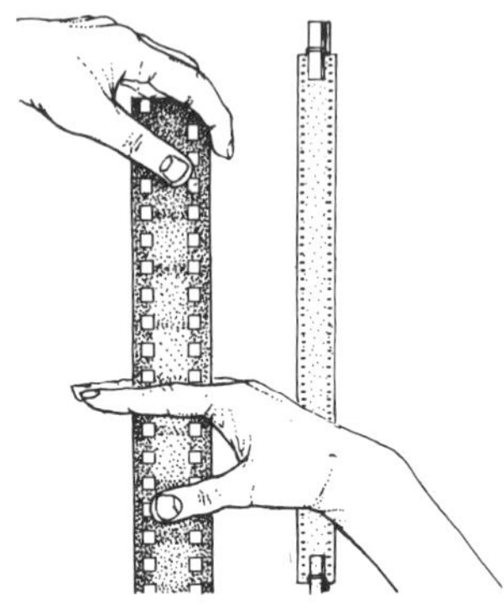

Rinse

If you intend to develop the film as soon as the developer is ready, it is a good idea to prepare a rinse of water at about 20°C (68°F) for use later. You need enough to fill and empty the tank twice.

Developer

Mix up carefully, following manufacturer's instructions. Use the thermometer as you go to aim for the exact temperature (roughly within a degree) you will need for development, which is 20°C (or 68°F).

You can raise or lower the temperature of the developer after it is mixed by using a hot water or ice-cube-in-water bath, but it takes time.

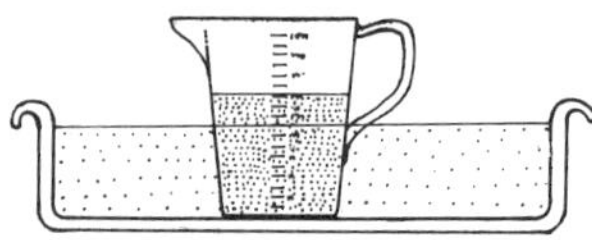

Leave the developer in the tank for the development time stated in the manufacturer's instructions, for the type of film you have at (normally) 20°C, agitate as per manufacturer's instructions, for example, 5 sec. every minute.

3. At the end of the development time pour out the developer, either to store or to throw away, according to manufacturer's instructions.
4. Fill with prepared rinse water at about 20°C. Empty ... Refill ... Empty.
5. Fill with fixer. After 30 sec., look at the film to see if there is any cloudiness on it.

Leave it in the fixer for twice as long as it took for this cloudiness to clear.

6. Pour fixer into bottle for reuse. Wash film in slow running water for 15 min., emptying once or twice.
7. Add a few drops of wetting agent to the final wash.

> **Alternative development**
> It is possible to develop a film in its own cassette. A 20-exposure 35 mm. film, with the first and last three frames left blank, is immersed in a beaker of monobath developer. The end of the film is fixed to the outside of the cassette with a rubber band, (leader cut off first). A dowel rod is inserted into the knob at the end of the cassette, and turned continuously during development. By careful counting, the two extreme positions of completely wound up and completely unwound can be avoided. There is no fixing stage with monobath development. (Wash and dry as normal.) There is a risk of uneven development.
> Monobath developer is not widely stocked at photo processing centers.

Contact printing

SETTING UP THE DARKROOM

Black a room out with polyethylene, curtains, or paint, etc. (Black plastic car covers can be bought quite cheaply for this.) A kitchen or bathroom is best, as running water is necessary.

You need a yellow safelight or safelight-bulb. Printing paper is not affected by a yellow safelight. You also need to be able to switch on the normal "white" light.

There should be a "dry area" for the exposing and a "wet area" for dishes, rubber gloves, print tongs, thermometer, etc., for processing.

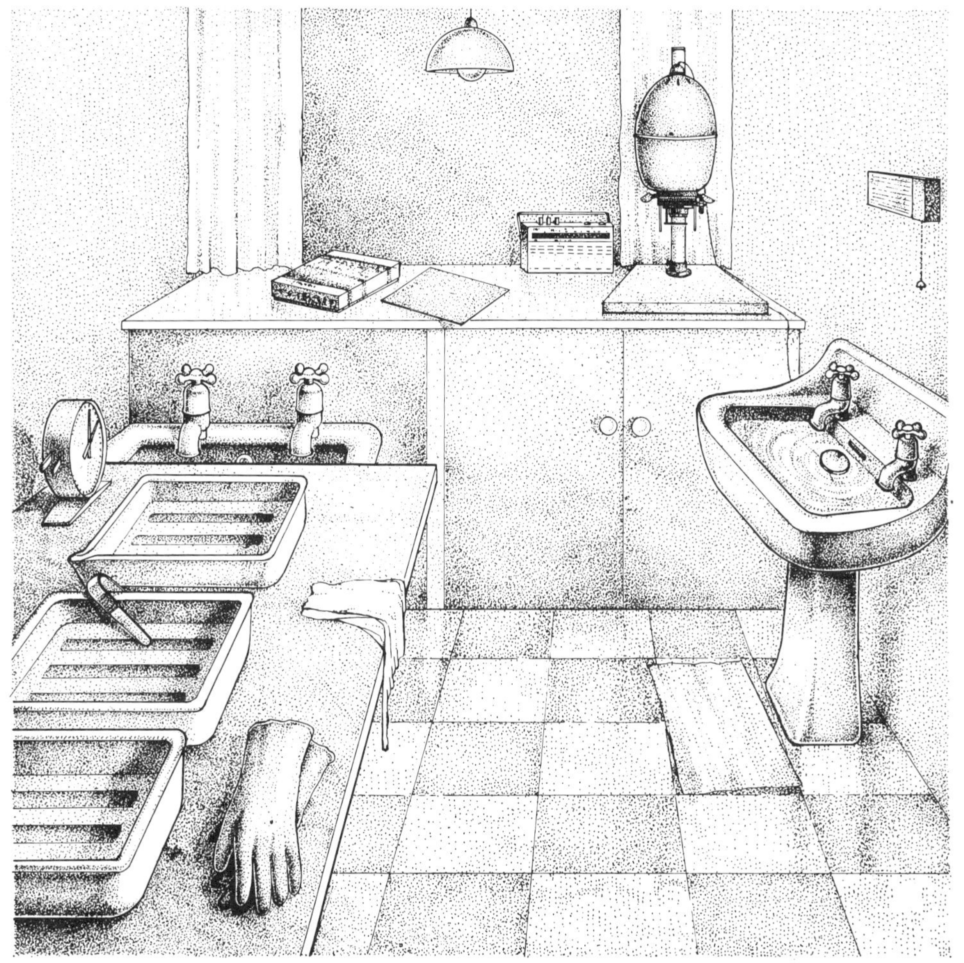

EQUIPMENT

1. An 8 in. x 10 in. sheet of glass, or contact frame.
2. An enlarger as a light source to expose the print, or a lamp with 15 watt bulb.

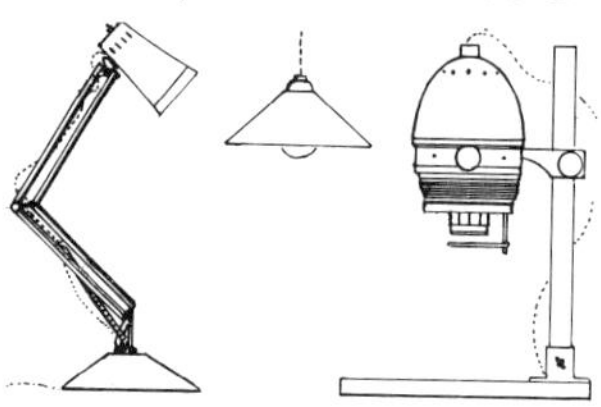

3. Three 8 in. x 10 in. darkroom dishes. (You can make them by pinning heavy-duty polyethylene to a frame, fruit-box, or seed trays.)

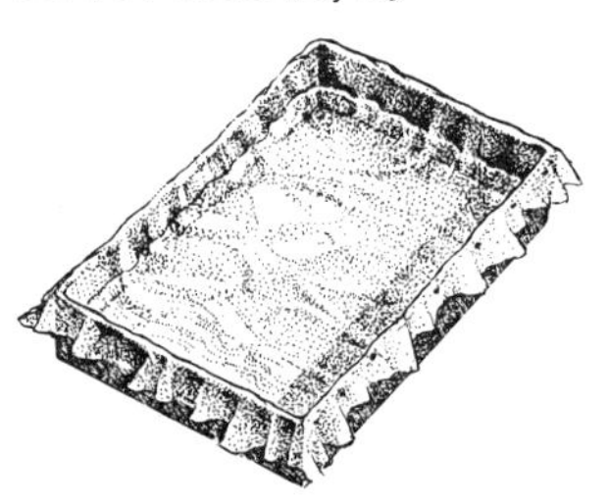

4. A place to wash prints, like a basin with a piece of plastic pipe as overflow.

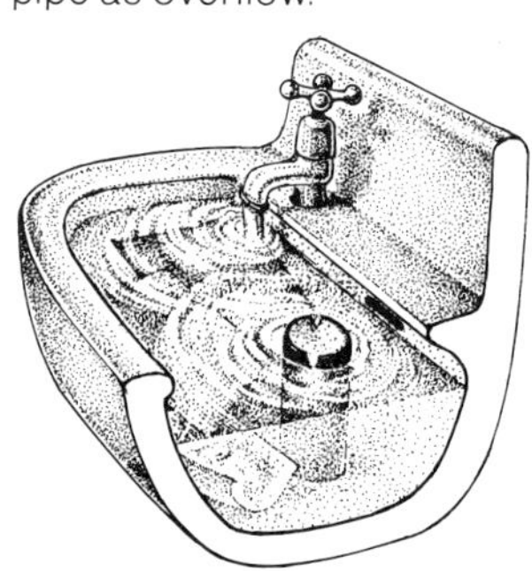

5. A towel and apron.
6. A darkroom clock, or any thing with a second hand.
7. A piece of card to use when making test strips.
8. A radio is nice – once you have gained experience!

MATERIALS

1. Resin coated printing paper is replacing the standard variety. It is easy to use and dries flat. A packet of ten sheets Grade 2 ("normal") 8 in. x 10 in. (20.3 cm. x 25.4 cm.) will do for a start. (Some manufacturers describe Grade 3 as "normal," in which case use this.) There are different surfaces, but try White Smooth Glossy.
2. Developer. A packet or bottle of paper developer; the cheapest works well.
3. Fixer. A packet or bottle of fixer. All are suitable for prints.

SETTING UP

Lay out three trays or dishes on the "wet area" or sink. Fill with mixed-up developer at 20°C, rinse water, and fixer, respectively, following manufacturer's instructions. Rinse and fixer can be cold.

MAKING THE TEST STRIP

White light off	■	□

1. Open printing paper. Place a sheet face up (the face is slightly sticky) under the exposing light or enlarger, which is still off.

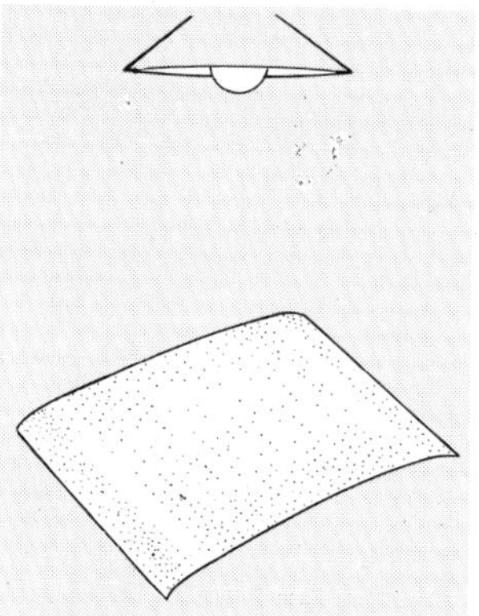

2. Lay out the negatives in rows shiny side up on the printing paper.

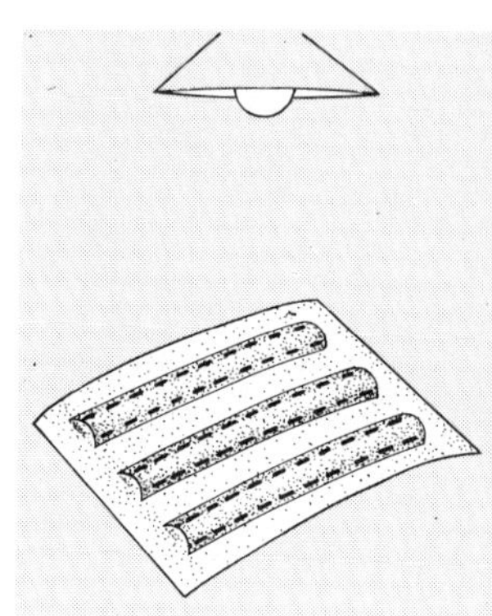

3. Place the sheet of clean glass carefully on top, pressing the negatives flat down onto the printing paper.

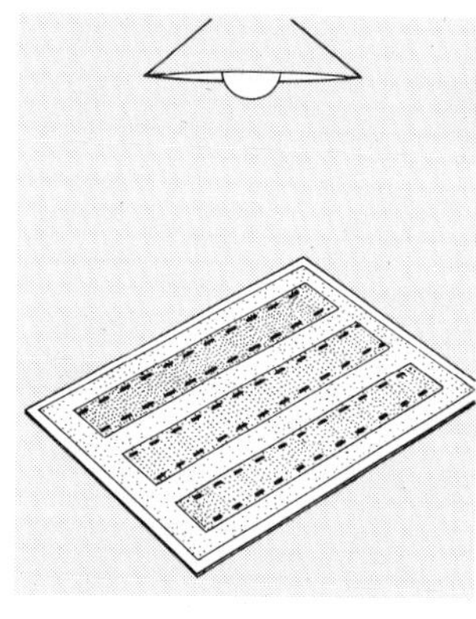

4. Switch on the enlarger or exposing light (if an enlarger is used, stop it down two stops, to give a four-second exposure. If you use a room light, divide this time and those that follow by 2 or 4, according to brightness.)

If you count to yourself "A thousand-and-one, a thousand-and-two, a thousand-and-three,' etc., you can count seconds accurately enough.

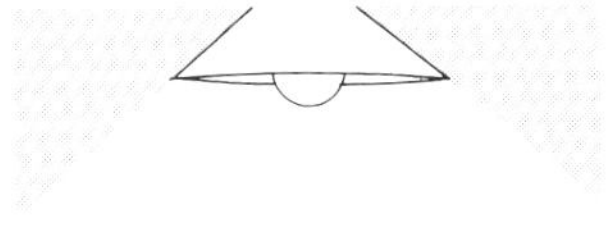

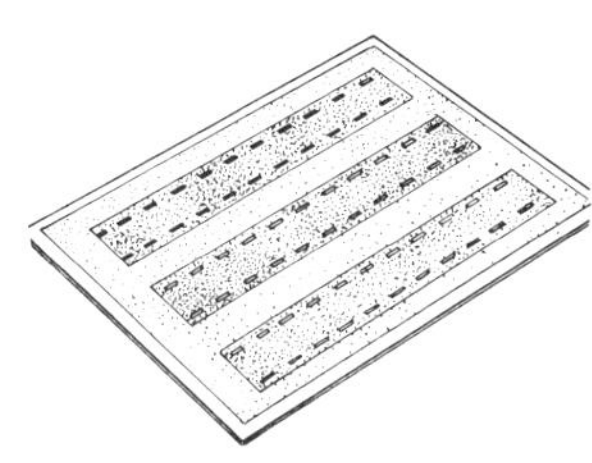

5. Switch off exposing light. Cover roughly one-quarter of the glass with a piece of stiff card.
6. Expose for four more seconds.

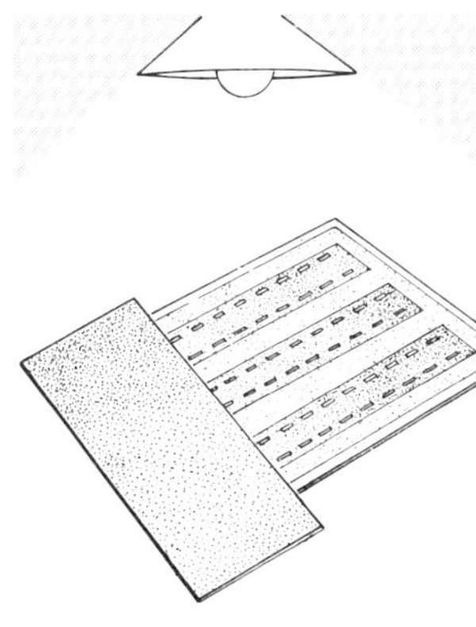

7. Move card to cover half of glass. Give 8 sec.
8. Cover three-quarters of glass. Expose 16 sec.

You have now exposed your contact test print in strips of 4, 8, 16, and 32 sec. (Notice that the exposure doubles between each step, just as

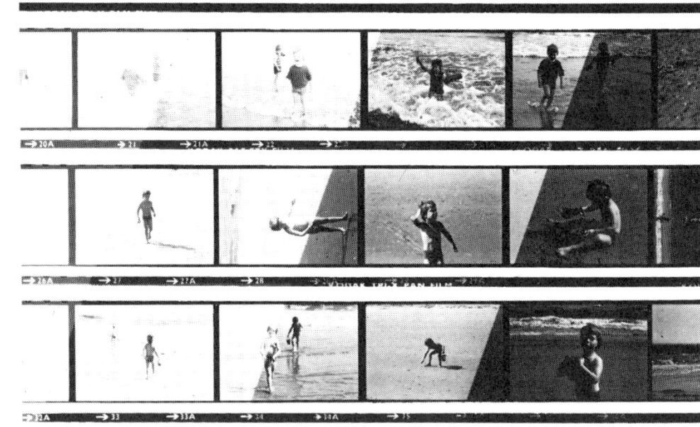

▲ *Contact test strip.*

the shutter speeds on a camera do.)
9. Remove glass and negatives; slide paper into developer, which must cover it, and start timer or note exact time on watch or clock.

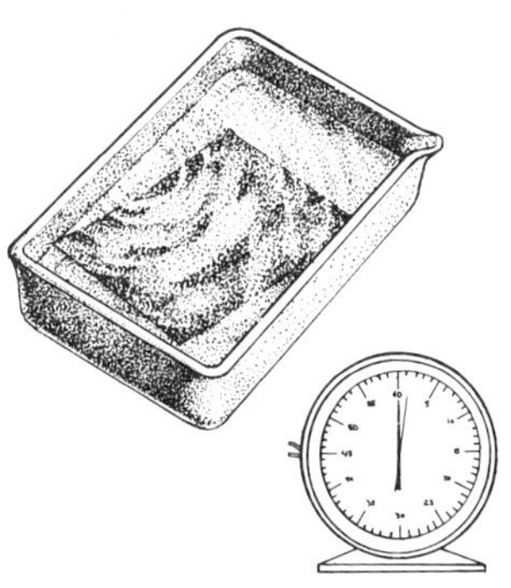

10. Develop for 1½ min. (resin coated paper), or 2 min. (standard paper), rocking gently. Even if print goes too dark, leave it in for the full time. Most wishy-washy gray prints are the result of incomplete development (or cold developer).
11. Rinse in second (rinse) dish. Drain for a few seconds.

12. Slide into fixative dish. Make sure it is covered.

White light on 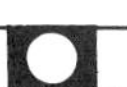

Examine your test strip print.
13. Choose the best exposure. If the whole sheet is either too light or too dark, change the brightness or closeness of the exposing light and make another test strip.

MAKING THE CONTACT PRINT

White light off

14. Repeat steps 1 – 12, but this time give the whole sheet the best exposure.

White light on 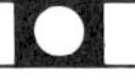

15. Leave prints in the fixer for about 10 min. (see manufacturer's instructions).
16. Wash in gently running water for 4 min. if resin coated, or 40 min. if standard paper.
17. Wipe drips off and lay out to dry. (Standard paper has to be dried in a print dryer or in blotting paper.)

Making enlargements

Equipment

The darkroom is basically the same as for contact printing.

1. An enlarger. This can be secondhand – or even, with a little ingenuity, homemade. It must be large enough to take your film size or larger. You may need to buy a new and better lens – which should be as good as the lens in your camera.
2. A masking frame is helpful, but not indispensable – you can simply mark out lines on the enlarger baseboard and use small weights on the extreme corners of the printing paper to hold it flat.

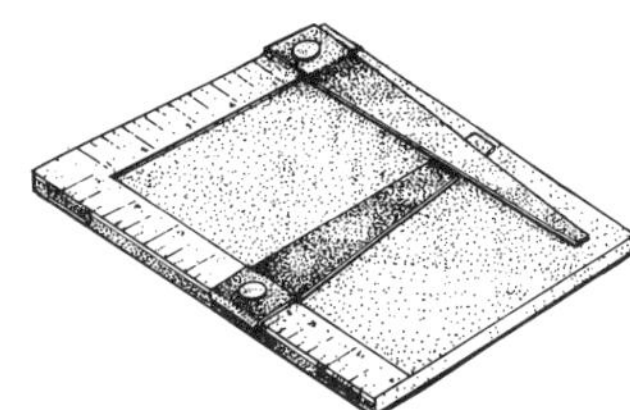

3. A rubber puffer-blower to blow dust off the negative and negative-carrier as you put the negative in.

Other equipment and materials are the same as for contact printing, except that you may find that you need to buy printing paper in a different grade than the Grade 2 suggested before.

PROCEDURE

1. Prepare chemicals as for contact printing.
2. Clean enlarger negative-carrier.
3. Blow any dust off negative and place it in the carrier. Mask off any clear area around negative. Move enlarger up or down column, refocusing as you go, until picture is the correct size. Focus carefully. An enlarger focusing aid enables you to focus on the grain for maximum sharpness.
4. Close down lens 2 to 3 stops and switch off. Turn on yellow safelight.

White light off

5. Place a strip of paper in frame and make a test strip as for contact printing. Try to include areas which should print to a maximum black.
6. Develop for a full 1½ min. at 20°C (2 min. standard paper). Don't take print out early: ask a friend to tie your hands behind your back!
7. Rinse and slide into fixer. Wash your hands if there is fixer on them. Check to ensure that paper packet is closed.

White light on 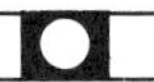

8. Assess test strip for correct exposure.

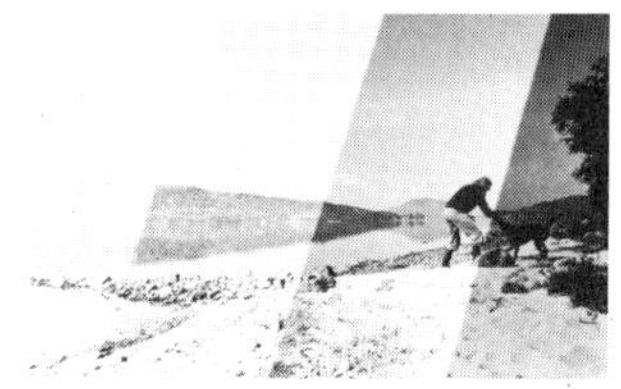

If you can't decide which exposure is best, remember that a "good" print should have some pure white and some pure black in it somewhere, however small. Take the exposure that just gives an area or point of pure black. If the whole strip is too dark or too light, close down the aperture or increase exposure accordingly.

White light off

9. Make a complete print at correct exposure, develop,

Grades of paper
The grade indicates the contrast of the paper. Grade 0 or 1 is soft or low contrast. Grade 2 or 3 is medium contrast. Grade 4 or 5 is very hard or high contrast. Normal negatives should print well on Grade 2 or 3. Use Grade 0 or 1 if your film is overdeveloped or the subject exceptionally contrasty. Use Grade 4 or 5 if your film is underdeveloped, underexposed or of very low contrast. (A high contrast print is one where much of the image is very black and white. A low contrast print is light and dark gray.)

rinse, and fix. Check to see that packet is closed and...

White light on 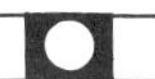

10. Assess print for exposure and contrast. Too dark or too light?
Have another look at your test strip and reassess exposure time.

Too hard or too soft?
If the print is too hard (contrasty) for your liking, change "down" one grade, e.g., to Grade 1 (soft).
If it is too soft (lacking in contrast) try Grade 3.
All this only applies if you developed the full time at 20°C, not if you took the print out early.

11. Now look at particular parts of the print. Are the faces a little dark, or the sky too light?

These can be corrected in a further print.

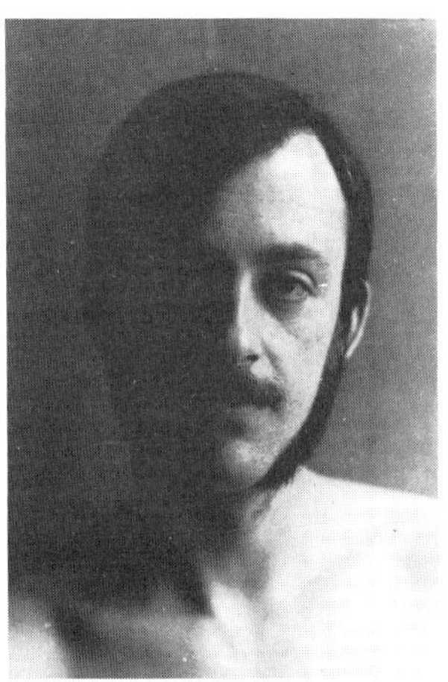

▲ **Dark print.**

▼ **Light print.**

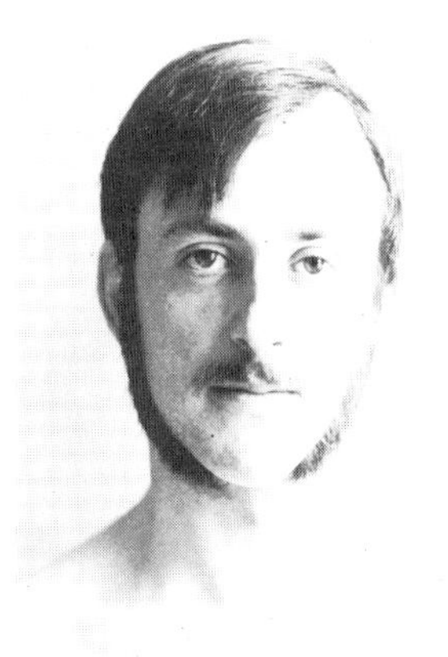

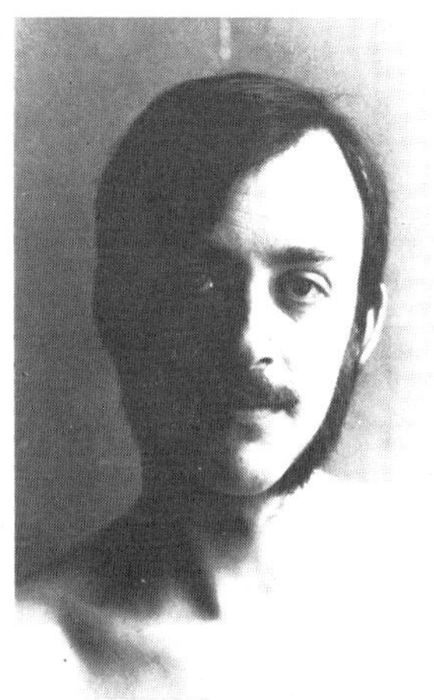

▲ **Hard print.**

▼ **Soft print.**

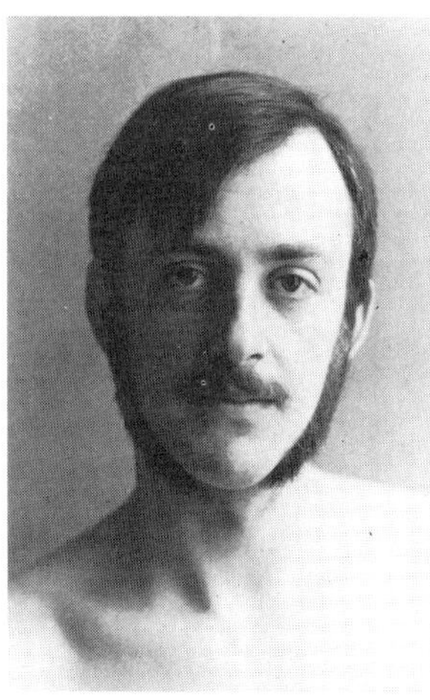

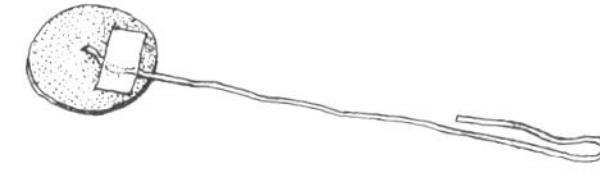

To lighten areas
Fix a piece of black paper to a length of stiff wire.

Use it to cut off some of the light from overly dark areas during, say, one-fifth of the exposure time. Keep it moving or you will be able to see an image of the wire on the print.

To darken areas
Make a hole with your hands or with paper to let light fall only on areas that are too light in tone. The amount of light varies from, say, an extra fifth of the basic time up to an extra exposure several times the basic one. Keep moving slowly, or the hole's shape will show.
12. When the prints have been in the fixative for about 10 min. you can put them to wash in gently running water. Wash and dry as for contact printing.
13. Use a very small paint brush and some black watercolor paint to fill in any white spots on the prints. The secret is to use minute quantities of paint on an almost dry brush. One tube of paint should be enough for the total readership of this book!

Reading pictures

Although photography has existed for nearly 150 years, only in the last twenty years or so has a coherent theory of criticism of its methods and language developed. Originally, photographic criticism was based on art criticism, early photographs being judged in comparison with paintings. Then people slowly began to realize that the content of a picture was one of its most important attributes.

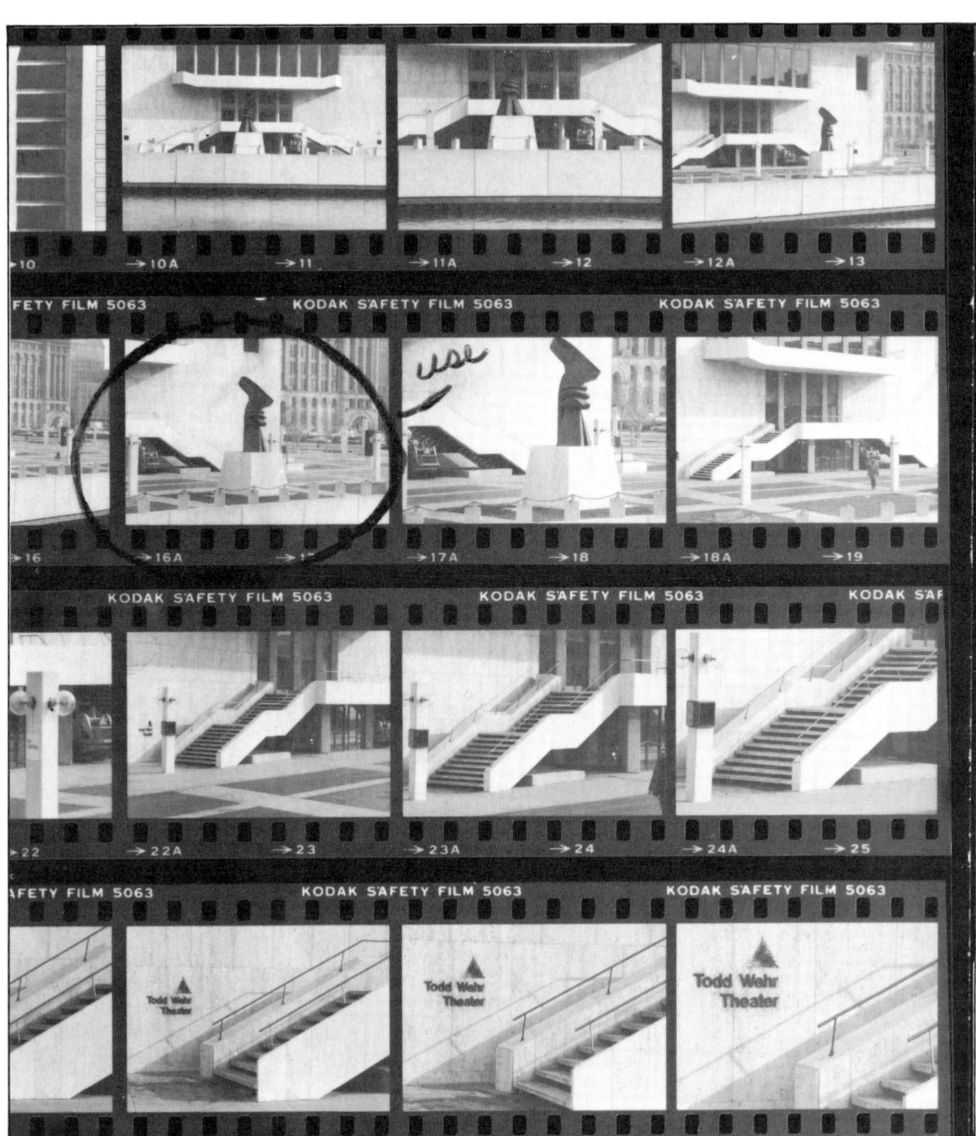

Nowadays there is much debate about the relative importance of content (what a picture is about), and form (how the information is presented). Fashions and responses change, so it is difficult to determine if a picture is well-composed or properly lit. It is also difficult to look at a picture and derive the maximum information from it. Nothing in our education has prepared us to do this systematically. Every culture has a different bias and each will encourage its members to see only certain things in pictures, as in life.

An American businessman will read the same picture differently from an Indian villager; a sociologist will see different information from a geologist. A child will see different information from an adult. The harder you look and think about most pictures the more you will get from them. Discussion with other viewers often helps with the process. This section is about learning to look at pictures more thoroughly and critically, and is about selecting and editing your own work. It also raises the question of what happens when you add written material to visual information.

Selection and editing

When you have made your contact prints or collected them from the photo processing center, study them carefully. Look at them through a magnifying glass and mark the ones you select for enlargement with a wax pencil or felt tip pen. Make yourself two L-shaped pieces of black card which can be used together as a mask when looking at a whole sheet.

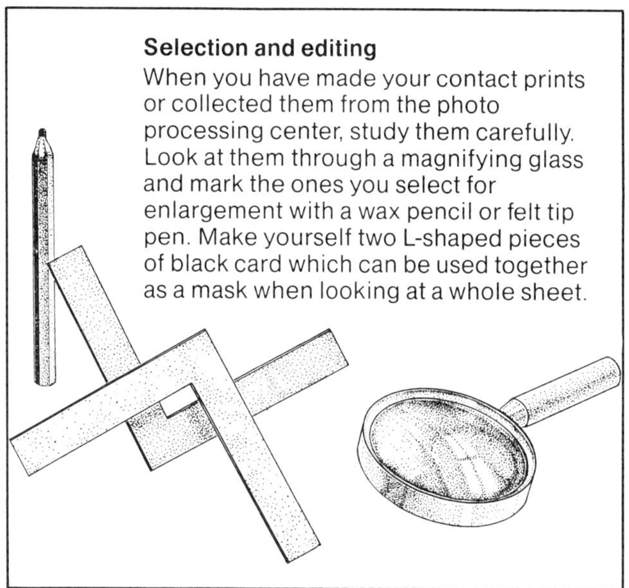

Selection and editing

When editing it is helpful to eliminate as much extraneous information as possible; if you try to view 36 pictures at once they all keep vying for your attention. If there are several versions of one picture, ask yourself which one best conveys the information you want to give.

Ideally all pictures should have interesting content and good technical quality. Sometimes you have to choose one or the other.

However characteristic the pose in a portrait, if the picture is so fuzzy or poorly lit that the person is unrecognizable, then the picture is useless. On the other hand, photographs of historic or dramatic events are often of very poor quality and unsharp. They are still used over and over again because nothing else exists that gives the same information – for example, the photograph of the assassination of President Kennedy. When it comes to photographing the family on the beach, though, there is little excuse for not taking control of both content and quality.

Try to imagine how other people will see the version you finally select. Remember that you will not necessarily be there to explain what happened before and after you pressed the shutter release. If the information isn't in the picture, no amount of looking at it will help viewers to see it.

Try not to be unfair or dishonest in selecting. It is easy to pick the one exposure out of 36 which shows a person looking miserable, just because it looks more dramatic or fits a particular idea or caption. You may want to crop or frame your picture differently. This can be done to emphasize the main subject and cut out unwanted details, e.g., a hand in the edge of the frame. Cropping can, however, change the meaning of a picture, so be careful. Some photographers always print the whole of their negatives (in fact some even print the edges of the negative so that we get the signal that they disciplined themselves before they pressed the shutter). However this requires lots of experience in framing at the time of taking the picture.

It is helpful to practice framing without actually taking any pictures. Use your viewfinder as if it were a window. Pretend you have just moved to a new home and you want to choose the ideal view from your window. Keep looking through your viewfinder until you are satisfied you have

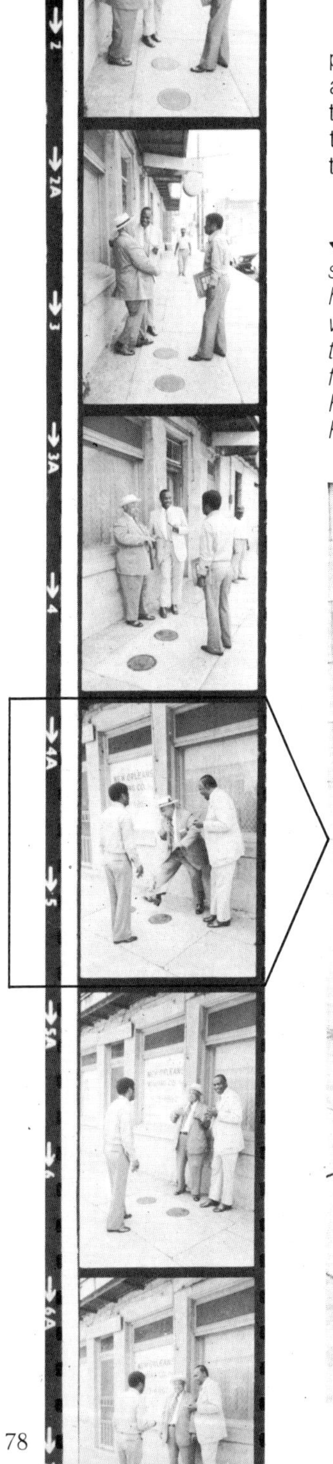

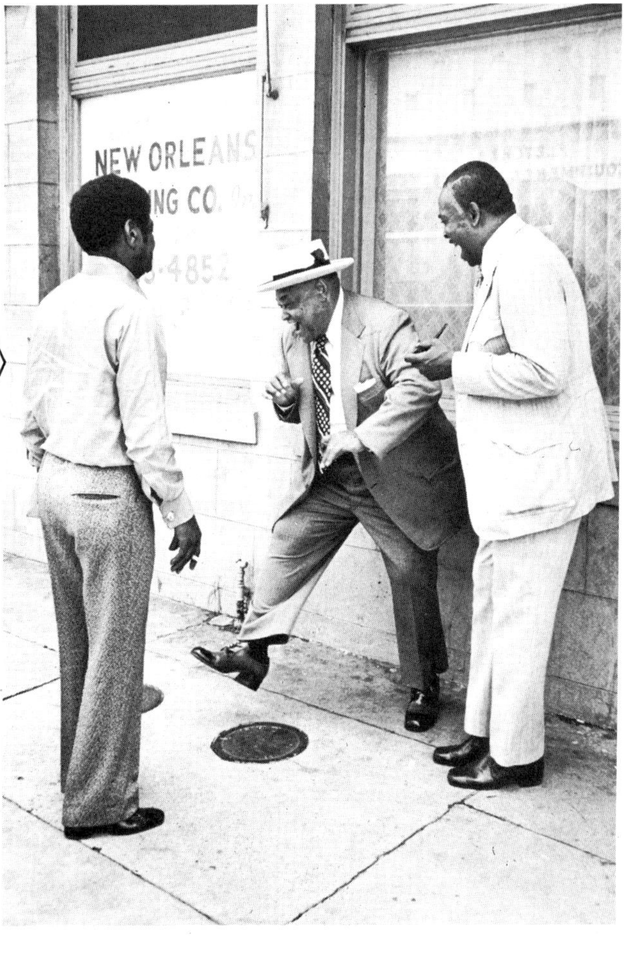

▾ *In this New Orleans street scene Valerie Wilmer has chosen the picture which most characterizes the meeting of these old friends, Cousin Joe Roosevelt Sykes and Rev. "Gatemouth" Moore.*

the best possible choice and could live with it for years.

The information you put with a picture – either in a newspaper caption or in a family album – can change meaning. Get the facts right. You may find you need to include a good deal of written material to make what you want to say quite clear. Some subjects are best explained in words with an explanatory photograph. Others come across best through pictures with short explanatory captions. Try to make sets of pictures up sometimes rather than always concentrating on single images. When building up a set or photo-essay try to vary the form of the pictures as well as covering all the content. Include close-ups, long shots, different viewpoints, and angles. Always

▼ *John Hilliard is an artist who sometimes uses photography. His work underlines the fact that every small element of a picture – including text – can affect meaning radically. This set is called "Ways of Death."*

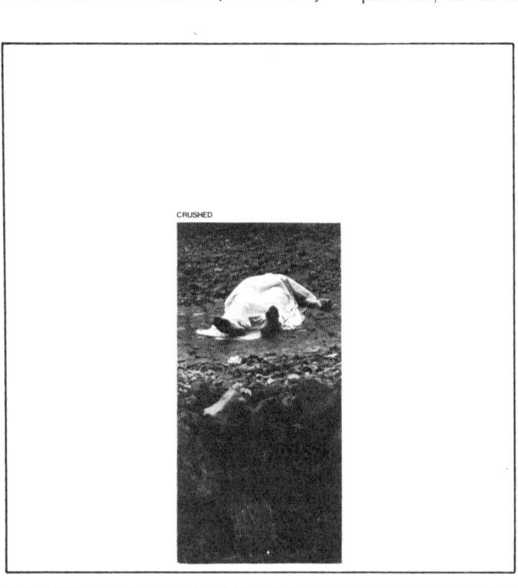

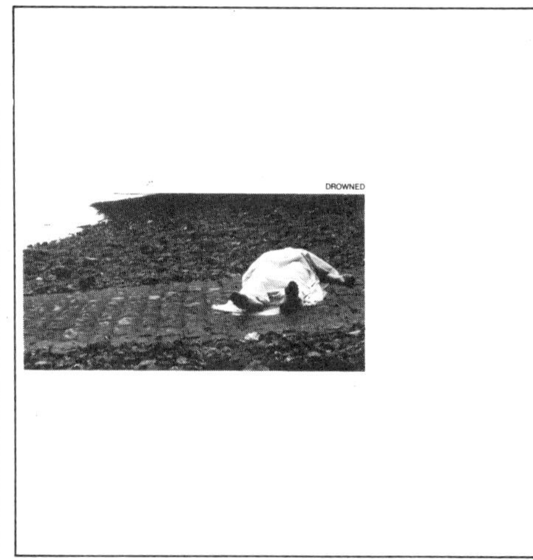

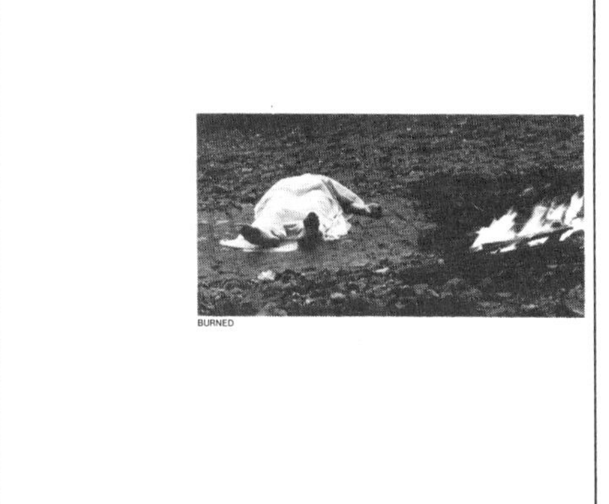

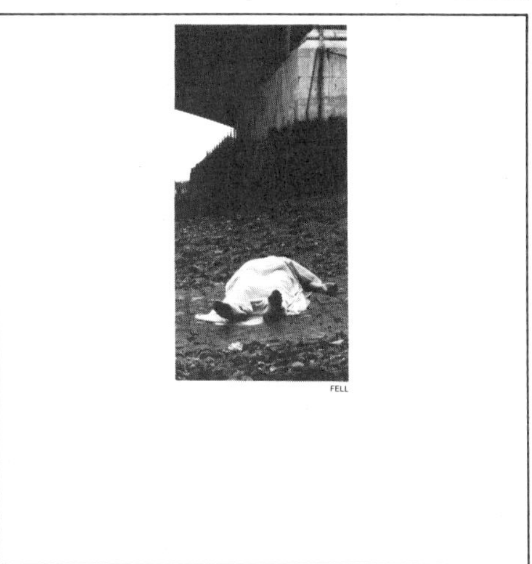

select each picture in relation to the others. It is no good having three versions of one aspect of the story just because three pictures are visually exciting, and then ignoring one important point because the picture is weak.

Once you have begun to work at building sets of pictures you will start to understand that taking a single picture out of a series can seriously distort or limit the message it conveys. Severe cropping of a picture or inaccurate accompanying text – even a single word – can result in actual dishonesty.

Study some of the extended books of photo-essays listed in the reference section. Compare the captions of identical pictures in different newspapers and magazines.

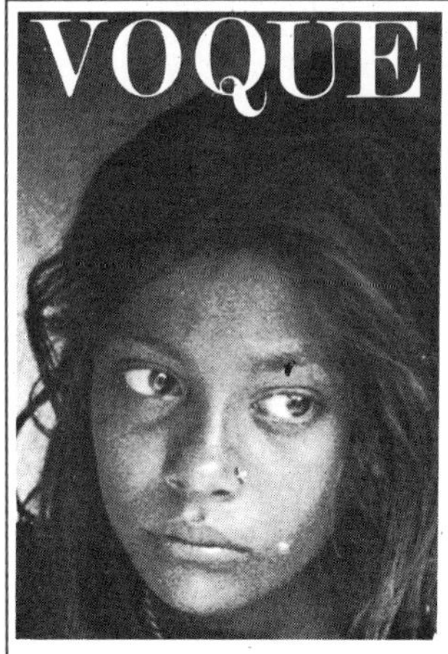

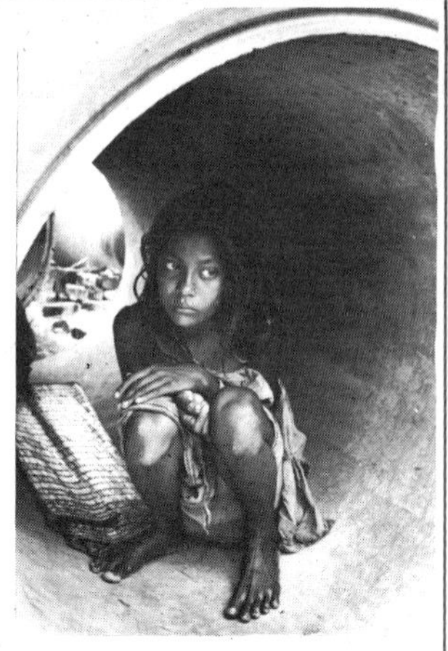

a) Cropping can alter the information a picture gives.

b) Text can reinforce inaccurate information.

c) Several pictures or a series may be necessary to give a full version of a situation.

The girl in these pictures was a refugee living in a drainpipe on the outskirts of Calcutta. She had fled from East Pakistan, now Bangladesh, during the border war of 1971. The drainpipes were standing on a swampy area that was awaiting drainage so that it could be used as a building site.

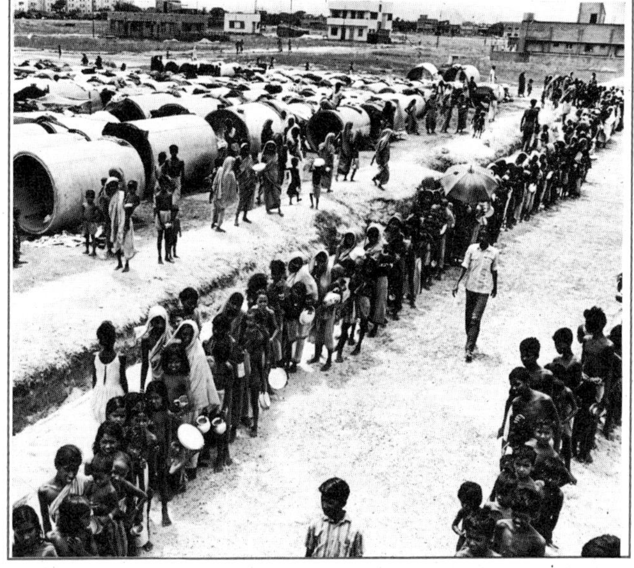

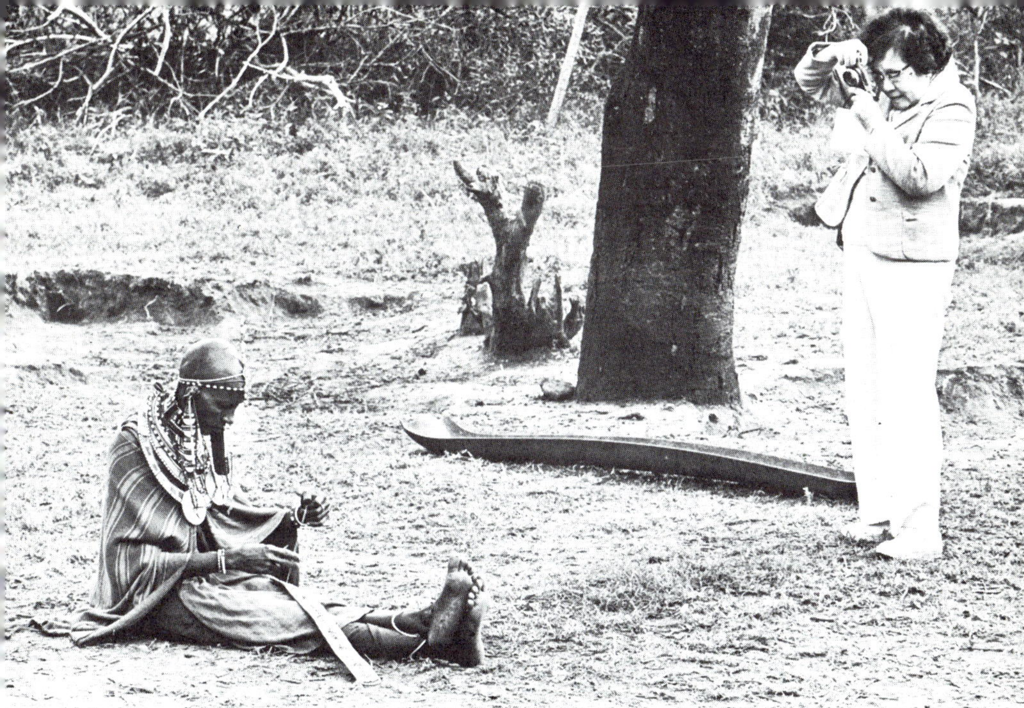

Reading pictures

Study this picture. These are some of the things that different people have said about it.

1. "What camera was it taken with?"
2. "This is a very interesting illustration of the effects of tourism in developing countries."
3. "What a beautiful woman. No wonder people want to photograph her."
4. "Did you set it up?"
5. "What horrible countryside. Where is it?"
6. "It is disgraceful that a photographer should make such a critical visual statement about the Japanese tourist. How does she know that the Japanese tourist is not an important sociologist? Did she ask?"
7. "What an interesting comparison of dress and costume."
8. "This photograph is about lack of communication."
9. "I don't like this picture, it is too confused."
10. "My mother has got a jacket just like that."
11. "What a shame the tourist got in the picture."
12. "What shutter speed did you use?"

Make a list of all the different comments people make about one of your own pictures. Often it will help you to see things in the picture you didn't see before. Sometimes the comments will infuriate you.

The picture was taken in Kenya in 1974 at a Masai village that is preserved for tourists to visit by minibus every weekday afternoon. The trip is organized and run by a German family that owns the farm in which the "village" is situated. The camera was a Pentax with a standard lens. Film was Tri-X and the exposure probably was 1/250 sec. f/11.

Projects

Visual lifeline

Sort out all the pictures in which you appear. Then, arrange them in date order (starting with the earliest on the left-hand side) in a long line across the room. In this way you can plot out a visual progression of the physical changes, fashions, styles, etc., through which you have passed.

If you have too many pictures, cut it down to a total of about thirty. Make a long concertina of paper splicing them together. Then lightly tack your visual lifeline onto sheets of paper and make what amounts to a pull-out book. Write dates or your age under each photograph. This is a project that can be done privately or with friends and family and is very revealing and will promote a lot of discussion. Leave blank pages at the end so that you can keep adding to it. This method can isolate vital information about ourselves that is usually hidden among the family pictures, especially as you have to turn the pages over, thus hiding everything which has gone before.

Encourage others to do the same thing. It is particularly interesting for brothers and sisters to do this separately and then place them one above each other. If there is, say, a five year gap, then stagger the beginning of the two lifelines to reflect this.

Identity scrapbook

These old photos can then be used in a different way. Taking an ordinary paper scrapbook, split it up into various sections, say a page for birth to 5 years then another for 5 to 10 years, teens, "coming of age," etc. Then stick photographs onto appropriate pages, leaving a blank page opposite each page used.

This page can then be filled in with the appropriate historical images from old newspapers, advertisements, and history books, even the books you read as a child (all obtainable from people's shelves, or from secondhand or junk shops very cheaply), gradually building up material over a period of time until you have covered all the previous years of your life. This can only be a long term project, but it is one in which you can involve any number of people. You can even include maps, documents, certificates, newspaper headlines – anything that will help to reconstruct a personal history, linked to a wider context by the juxtapositioning of images on opposite pages.

Old advertisements and film stills will be particularly revealing and will often mirror fashions, make-up, and hairstyles featured in snapshots. Such books are a good focal point for family discussion and a valuable means of getting children to make their own versions, using current pictures of themselves, added to what they think is relevant from current media images, comic books, and postcards. Projects like this can help to bring about a closer understanding between different generations. That quiet old grandmother who only gets a visit once a month might suddenly turn out to have lived through two world wars, the Depression, the Roaring Twenties, etc. Also, speculation about what may happen in the future will be as interesting as digging up the past.

Montage

If a personal scrapbook is too boring (or revealing) then something for instant fun is to scour magazines for pictures of how we would like to look (or hate to look), cut them out, and then superimpose our bodies onto real photographs of people we know, adding suitable speech bubbles.

Experiment

Load black and white film into your camera, use it for your private photography, develop and print it yourself, decide never to show it to anyone, and ultimately destroy it. This may sound like a pointless exercise but it will show you how your photographs might differ if no one else was ever intended to see them.

Landmarks in the development of photography

▼ *George Eastman, who started the Kodak company, photographed with and by the first box camera in 1890. The film used with the camera gave 100 circular negatives. Once the roll was completely exposed the whole camera was mailed back to the manufacturers who boasted, "You press the button, we do the rest."*

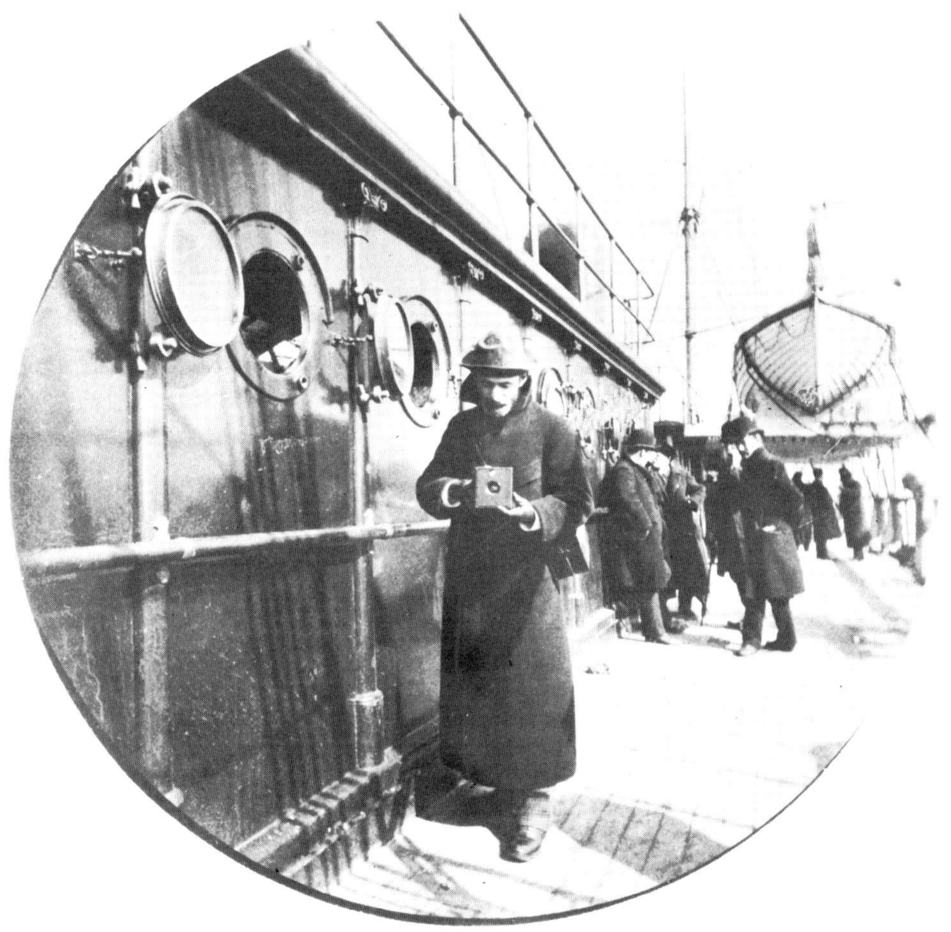

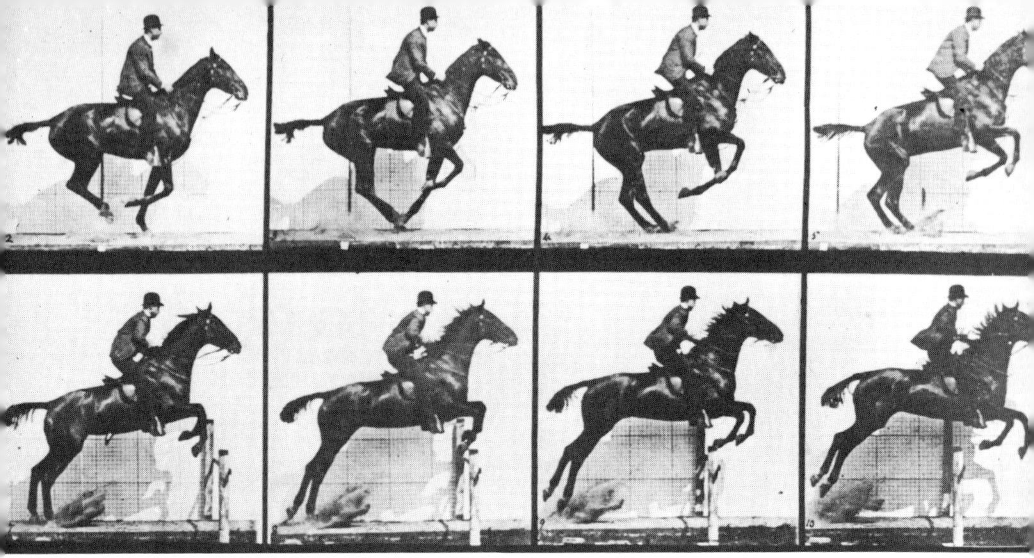

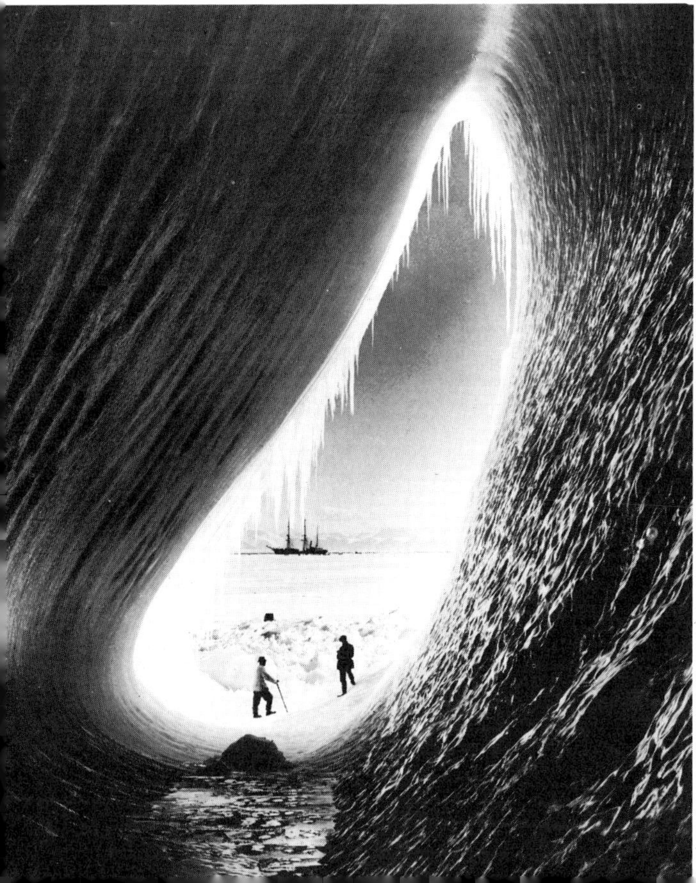

▲ One of Edward Muybridge's sequences of pictures taken to illustrate animal movement in the 1880s. These were taken on a series of cameras. His experiments led to the development of the motion picture camera.

◀ Photograph from a documentary series taken on an Antarctic expedition in 1908 by Herbert Ponting.

▶ Robert Capa's photograph of the D-Day landing is a dramatic record of a historically important event. It is also an example of the effect of unavoidable blur adding to the atmosphere of the moment.

DATES

1826 Nicéphore Niepce. First successful photograph from nature (France).

1839 Daguerre. First practical system for producing photographs, Daguerreotypes (France).

1839 Fox Talbot. The negative/ positive system which is the basis of modern photographic systems (GB Calotypes).

1840 The boom in professional portrait studios starts.

1851 Scott Archer. The collodion wet plate process. Plates were wet at the time of exposure (GB)

1851 Stereoscopic photographs and equipment first marketed.

1855 Roger Fenton. Took wet plate photographs of the Crimean War (GB).

1856 Rejlander. First large scale photo-montage.

1860 Brady. Recorded the American Civil War.

1868 Dry plates invented. Modern film is based on these.

1868 Ducos du Hauron demonstrated the principles of color photography.

1873 *Daily Graphic* printed the first photo-illustration.

1883 Muybridge's series of horses galloping. These led to the development of cinematography.

1888 The first Kodak roll film box camera.

1904 The first daily newspaper illustrated exclusively with photographs – the *Daily Mirror.*

1924 Ermanox and Leica 35mm lightweight cameras produced. The first readily available miniature cameras.

1931 First photoelectric exposure meter.

1935 Kodachrome, the first color film for miniature cameras. Polaroid Land Camera that produces prints in 10 seconds.

1970 First fully automatic exposure miniature cameras and electronic flash guns.

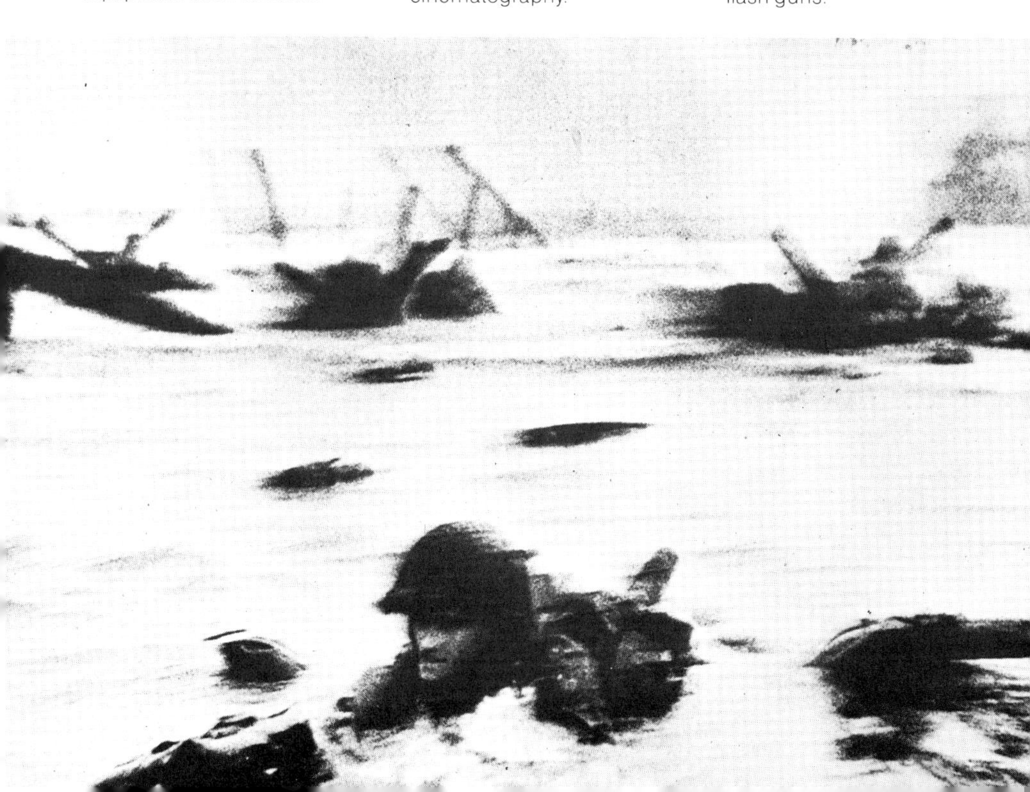

What film?

Film is a gelatin strip coated with a light-sensitive emulsion. This is wound through a camera one frame at a time so that individual exposures are made along the film length. These exposures cause chemical changes in the emulsion. When the emulsion is treated with special chemicals, these changes are recorded as negative images.

Cartridges: slot into camera back, programming the camera with film speed.

Roll film: has a paper backing which must be threaded onto the camera take-up spool and advanced to the start of the film.

Cassettes: the leader is threaded onto the take-up spool and 20, 24, or 36 exposures made before the film is wound back into the cassette.

BLACK AND WHITE FILM

Slow films need longer exposure or larger apertures, but they record very fine detail. The final print looks very smooth, as the image is not visibly broken into grainy stipple except at very great enlargement. Ilford Pan F and Kodak Panatomic-X are examples. The camera is often placed on a tripod when using them.

Medium speed films such as Kodak Plus X and Ilford FP4 are still very sharp and have fine grain. They are more practical for general use, but are still not really fast enough for use by available light indoors.

Fast films such as Kodak Tri-X, Ilford HP5, and Agfapan 400 are very good for most purposes. They are ideal for available-light work and have acceptable grain and sharpness if carefully processed. Tri-X developed in D76 1 + 1 is widely used as a basic black-and-white film.

Ultra fast films such as Kodak 2475 Recording Film are very grainy and not very sharp. They produce a result under very poor light conditions, but the grain is so coarse that the prints look as if they have been made on sandpaper. (They are also used to produce an "arty" effect.)

Whichever film you choose, it is worthwhile to get used to it rather than changing film types frequently. Unless you find the grain unpleasant, a fast film is a good choice as it gives the most possibilities.

COLOR FILM

Transparency (reversal) films (for color slides).
These also come in a range of speeds.

Slow films Kodachrome 25 is the sharpest film and also gives excellent color rendition.

Medium speed films: Kodachrome 64 is sharper than most other films because the color dyes do not have to be contained in the film – they are added during development. Ektachrome 64 and Agfachrome 64, though not as sharp, give excellent results. In fact, the high cost of setting up a production line to manufacture films means that it is simply not worthwhile producing anything second-rate. Each film has a subtly different color response; some photographers swear by one, some by another.

Fast films: These range from ASA 100 to ASA 400. Examples include Fujichrome 100, Ektachrome 200, and Ektachrome 400. These do not produce as much detail as some of the slower films. However, there have been vast improvements in high-speed color films, and in normal usage the difference in sharpness between an ASA 25 film and an ASA 400 film is not great.

Transparency films for use in tungsten (artificial) lighting: Ektachrome Type B film is balanced for use in artificial light. If used in daylight, or with flash, it will come out blue. ASA 125.

Neg./Pos. film: If you want color prints you need to use a Neg./Pos. film such as Kodacolor, Vericolor, Agfa CNS, or Fujicolor. The quality of the results depends not so much on the film as on the processing. If prints come out of the machine looking wrong, they should be reprinted. Some processors take more care than others.

Inside information

Equipment and news: The best way to find out what equipment (new or second-hand) is available, and from whom, is to read one of the numerous photographic magazines. They will also keep you up to date on what is going on in various areas of photography. Two magazines in particular, *Modern Photography* and *Popular Photography*, have monthly test reports on cameras and other photographic equipment. In addition, these magazines are filled with advertisements from camera stores that sell equipment at discount prices.

Rentals: For special occasions it is possible to rent cameras, lenses, or other equipment. You can also rent studios, models, and every imaginable sort of prop for a photograph. Many retail camera stores have a rental department. You can also get books listing where to get what, but the simplest place to look is the Yellow Pages of the telephone directory.

Slide making: You can easily make slides from your own photographic prints, magazines, artwork, or other illustrations. You simply photograph each item separately on a suitable film: for b/w, Agta Gevaert Dia Direct; for color, Kodachrome 25 or 64. After exposure, send it to the manufacturers, who will process it and return it as positive transparencies or slides. It is important that the camera is steady – use a tripod and cable release. The illustration should be evenly lit – work outside or near a large window. The back of the camera could be as parallel to the illustration as possible. Try to avoid reflections on the surface of the illustration. You may need close-up lenses or extension rings to copy small originals. Using these methods you can make slide shows from mixed materials on any subject.

Copying: You can copy old photographs, illustrations, etc.,

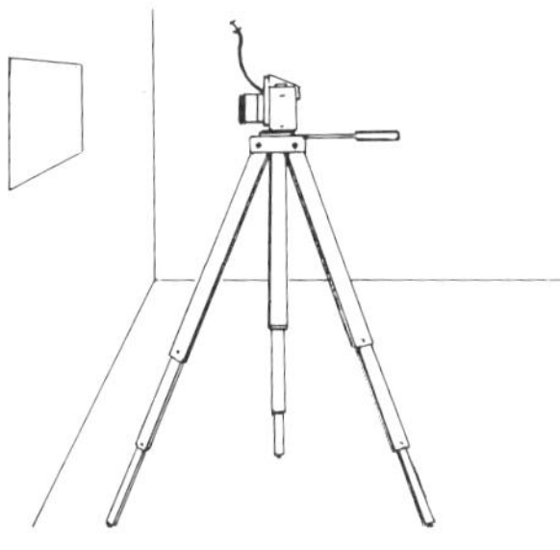

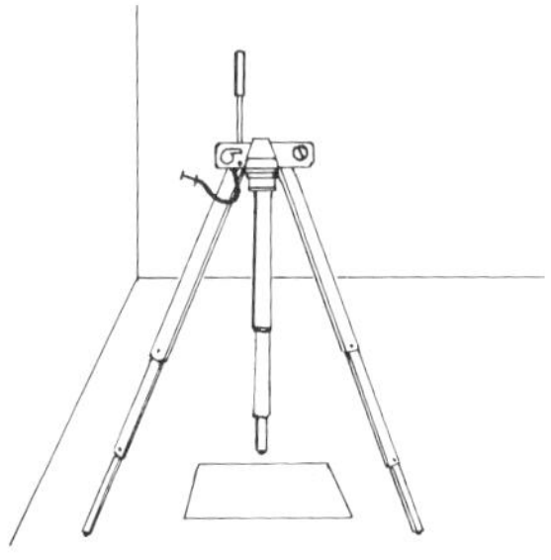

to use for exhibitions or information. Set the camera up the same as for slide making but choose a slow negative film like Kodak Panatomic X. Process it and you will obtain negatives from which you can print.

Photography abroad: If you take your camera abroad try to remember the following.

1. If the camera is expensive take the purchase receipt with you so that you can prove it was bought in this country when you want to bring it back through customs.
2. Try to store cameras and equipment in a cool place. Tropical heat can damage films.
3. Do not allow your films to be X-rayed at airports, as this may fog them. Lead-lined bags are sold to protect against this, but they are not foolproof.
4. In many countries photography is forbidden, especially near military installations, bridges, or ports. You could be arrested for taking an innocent snapshot.
5. Recommended exposures may vary in extreme conditions, e.g., snow and sunlit beaches should be given ½ to 1 stop more than normal.
6. Especially when you are near the equator, avoid shooting in sunlight between 11:00 A.M. and 3:00 P.M. if possible. The overhead lighting gives harsh results.

Processing labs: Rather than taking your films or printing to the drugstore, you can take them to a local processing lab. This is often cheaper and better, but check prices first, as some are very expensive.

Most color film can go back to the manufacturer for processing but the advantages of an independent lab are that you will get the pictures back quicker and can have the speed of the film modified, e.g., pushed from ASA 400 to ASA 800. This, of course, costs extra and may change the color balance.

Courses

There are many different ways of learning photography. You can buy a camera and teach yourself, learn from others at a club or co-op, or go to evening or part-time classes.

The number of institutions that offer instruction in photography increased greatly in the 1970s. Some colleges and universities – Rochester Institute of Technology, for example – offer degrees with a specialization in photography. Other institutions – such as junior colleges, photography schools, the YMCA and YWCA, and camera clubs – offer evening study courses. In addition, individual photographers often hold short courses or workshops.

One can find many of these organizations in the Yellow Pages of the telephone book. Also, photography magazines often list courses of instruction in issues published prior to the beginning of a school year or semester. But perhaps the most convenient way to find out about all instruction opportunities is by contacting a local camera club.

Grants

Various groups and schools give grants for photographic work. The donors and the amounts are subject to periodic change, so the best way to find out what grants are available is through listings obtained through educational institutions. The following list is a start.

Ford Foundation, 320 East 43rd Street, New York, NY 10017. The foundation gives grants to organizations as well as to individuals.

John Simon Guggenheim Memorial Foundation, 90 Park Avenue, New York, NY 10016. This foundation supports both projects and study in photography.

National Endowment for the Arts, 805 15th Street, Washington, D.C. 20506. The NEA gives various kinds of aid to individuals and organizations.

Useful addresses

Any list of useful addresses would be many pages long. In addition, because of the continuing rapid growth of the field of photography, such a list would quickly go out of date. The best source for addresses of all kinds are the photographic periodicals. Magazines such as *Modern Photography* and *Popular Photography* report on and describe all phases of photography. These magazines cover picture taking, exhibitions, contests and awards, instruction, equipment, repairs, and many other subjects. The magazines often give addresses so that readers can further pursue those subjects on their own.

Local chapters of The American Society of Photographers in Communications (ASMP) are good sources of photo information.

Probably the biggest single source of information is the Eastman Kodak Company. Kodak has publications on almost every facet of photography. Their publications range from short pamphlets to hardbound books. Many are available in photo supply stores, but all can be obtained directly from Kodak. An index can be obtained by writing to:
Eastman Kodak, Department 412-L, Rochester, NY 14650.

Galleries

With the tremendous increase in the number of photographs being taken, it is only logical that there would be an increase in the number of photography exhibitions. In the past, art museums and galleries had occasional photo exhibits. Now many of these institutions have permanent photograph collections.

But what is more important to the average picture taker is the growing number of organizations that exhibit works of unknown photographers. In many cities, for example, small galleries are springing up in the neighborhoods. In addition, institutions such as universities, libraries, and businesses have exhibitions. What this means is that there are opportunities for unknown but talented photographers to have their work shown to the public. It also means that the public has more opportunities to view the works of more photographers – known or unknown.

The following list is not meant to be comprehensive; these are a few of the best known photographic galleries. Their literature will give a person an idea of the scope of photograph exhibitions in the United States.

International Center of Photography, 1130 Fifth Avenue, New York, NY 11028.

Light Gallery, 1018 Madison Avenue, New York, NY 10021.

Neikrug Galleries, Inc., 224 East 68th Street, New York, NY 10021.

Nikon House, 437 Madison Avenue, New York, NY 10022.

The Witkin Gallery, Inc., 243 East 60th Street, New York, NY 10022.

International Museum of Photography, George Eastman House, Rochester, NY 14607.

Light Impressions, 8 South Washington Street, Rochester, NY 14614.

Self-publishing

Self publishing is hardly a new concept (poets and writers have been doing it for centuries), but, it is an exciting step forward if you want your work to reach a wider audience. There are several ways in which you can do this, starting with simple postcards, moving on to posters and small books or folios.

The best thing about self-publishing is that it gives you complete control over how your work is used: the layout, typesetting, and printing. Probably the easiest beginning is a short run of postcards. This way you can concentrate on one really good image, which merely needs a caption.

When you venture into self-publishing it is best to approach several printers to compare prices before you take the plunge. Once you've found your friendly printer he or she can explain to you what type of contrast and tone range you need in your photograph in order to get the maximum quality in the reproduction process. Before you start worrying about what to do with a hundred postcards, your mind will have already moved on to something more ambitious. Perhaps you might need to make a poster. When making a poster you can do the whole printing process yourself, from layout to silk screen printing.

Many community centers have now set up print workshops where skills are passed on. Classes are also run in nightschool and adult education institutes (if not, you can ask for a class to be set up if there are enough of you to warrant it). Remember, if you go to a professional printer that the longer the print run the cheaper each individual sheet of printing will be. You will need to show the printer a mock-up of your pictures and text, or if you are really ambitious you can presstype directly onto white paper to the exact layout you require. Photographs can then be reduced to size to fit the gaps and a plate made of the whole thing. If you print it yourself, the bulk of the cost will be the paper, so keep your eyes open for cheap sources. Remember that your printer can give you a great deal of information in the planning stages that can save you frustration and cost later.

Some photographers and publishing groups have also self-published and marketed their own work in book form, often as part of local history and educational projects. The majority of such work would never have seen the light of day but for the devotion and hard work of those involved, because self publishing can seldom do more than break even financially.

Once you have tasted the pleasure of seeing your work in multiple form, and shared it with friends and family, sent it as Christmas cards or bookmarks (or even sold it) you will have moved toward a broader understanding of how the process of choosing and cropping images for maximum effect works. You may also learn how certain pictures work better with a particular typeface, how pictures can cancel each other out by being too cluttered with detail, or can raise contradictions.

A book that outlines self-publishing is: *The Publish-It-Yourself Handbook*, edited by Bill Henderson, Harper Colophon Books.

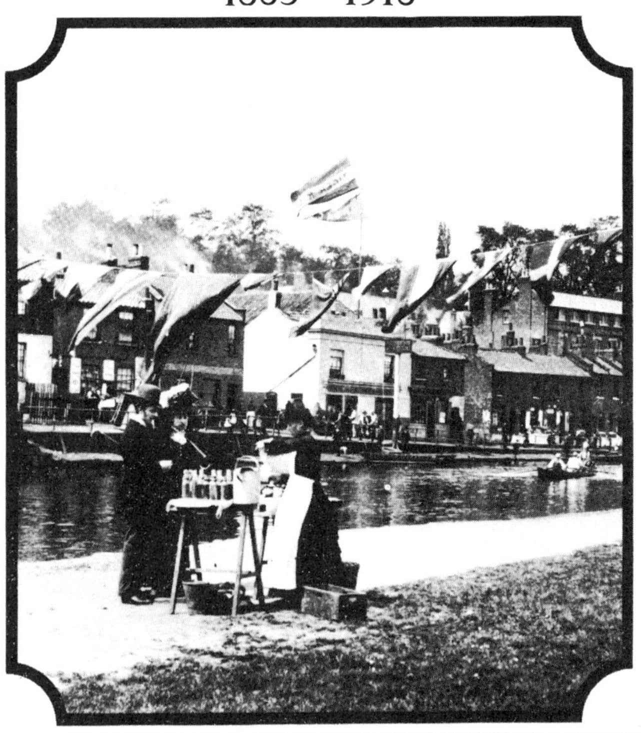

◄ *Centerprise, an alternative publishing project and community bookshop in London, has a programme of producing books of local poetry and people's writings, illustrated with old and new photographs. They have established an excellent working relationship with a local printer and have recently gone into a second printing of their book* A Hackney Camera, *compiled from local albums and archives. Their work is so popular that it is now used in local schools.*

Book list

REFERENCE

A Concise History of Photography, Helmut and Alison Gernsheim, Grosset and Dunlap.

The History of Photography from 1839 to the Present Day (revised edition), Beaumont Newhall, Museum of Modern Art.

Kodak Black-and-White Darkroom Dataguide, Eastman Kodak publication R-20.

Kodak Color Dataguide, Eastman Kodak publication R-19.

Life Library of Photography, Time-Life Books. This is a 17-volume set that covers the main categories in photography. Some of the titles include: *The Camera, Light and Film, The Print, The Art of Photography,* and *Photographing Children.*

GENERAL

The Craft of Photography, David Vestal, Harper and Row.

Darkroom Techniques, (two volumes), Andreas Feininger, Prentice-Hall.

Looking at Photographs, John Szarkowski, Museum of Modern Art.

101 Experiments in Photography, Richard D. Zakia and Hollis N. Todd, Morgan and Morgan.

Photographers on Photography, Nathan Lyons, Prentice-Hall.

Principles of Composition in Photography, Andreas Feininger, Amphoto.

Photography, A Handbook of History, Materials and Processes, Charles Swedlund, Holt, Rinehart and Winston.

Successful Photography (revised edition), Andreas Feininger, Prentice-Hall.

BOOKS OF PHOTOGRAPHS

Alfred Stieglitz: An American Seer, Dorothy Norman, Random House.

The Americans, Robert Frank, Grove Press.

Andre Kertész: Sixty Years of Photography 1912-1972, Grossman.

Ansel Adams: Images 1923-1974, New York Graphic Society.

The Appalachian Photographs of Doris Ullman, Amphoto.

Barbara Morgan, Morgan & Morgan.

Berenice Abbott Photographs, Horizon Press.

Deja-Vu, Ralph Gibson, Lustrum Press.

Dorothea Lange, Doubleday.

East 100th Street, Bruce Davidson, Harvard University Press.

Edward Weston: Fifty Years, Ben Maddow, Aperture.

The Eye of Eisenstaedt, Alfred Eisenstaedt, Viking.

The Family of Man, Edward Steichen, Simon & Schuster.

The Family of Woman, Grosset & Dunlap.

Imogen Cunningham, University of Washington Press.

Julia Margaret Cameron: Her Life & Photographic Work, Helmut Gernsheim, Aperture.

A Life in Photography, Edward Steichen, Doubleday.

Paul Strand: The Years 1915-1968, Aperture.

W. Eugene Smith: His Photographs & Notes, Aperture.

Walker Evans, New York Graphic Society.

Witness to Our Time, Alfred Eisenstaedt, Viking.

The World of Atget, Berenice Abbott, Horizon Press.

The World of Cartier-Bresson, Henri Cartier-Bresson, Viking.

Wynn Bullock: Photography— A Way of Life, Morgan & Morgan.

Glossary

Agitation: term used for various methods of keeping solution or sensitized material moving during processing.
Aperture: see f/number
ASA Speed: see film speed
"B" setting: on this setting, the shutter stays open as long as the shutter release is held down.
Cable release: flexible extension to shutter release. Reduces camera shake, e.g., at start of long exposure on a tripod.
Cartridge: latest type of light-tight holder for miniature film. Cannot be reloaded, and film does not need rewinding after exposure.
Cassette: light-tight metal or plastic container to hold length of film (usually 35mm). During exposure film is wound out of cassette, ultimately having to be rewound into cassette before opening back of camera. Can be reloaded for further use in some instances.
Coating: a thin film applied to the front of a lens to absorb extraneous light. Coating reduces flare and brightens the image. See also multi-coating.
Computerized flash: flash that has a built-in photocell to give correct exposure automatically.
Contact frame: holds negatives flat in contact with paper for making contact prints. Also called print frame.
Contact print: a print made by placing the negative(s) in direct contact with sensitized material.
Contrast: the ratio of dark to light (shadows to highlights) in a negative, transparency or print.
Convex lens: one which causes light rays to converge.
Depth of field: the amount of the subject that is sharp in front of and behind the point focussed on.
Depth of focus: the amount that the film plane can be moved to and from the lens while keeping the image sharp.
Developer: a mixture of chemicals that changes silver halide that has been exposed to light into a visible image formed of black metallic silver particles.
Differential focus: difference in sharpness produced by shallow depth of field.
Dry mounting: a method of mounting prints, (interleaved with dry-mounting tissues) onto board by the application of heat.
Electronic flashgun: portable unit giving a short, bright flash of light. Using a capacitor and gas-filled tube, it can be recharged and fired thousands of times. See also flash synchronization.
Emulsion: suspension of light-sensitive salts, usually coated on film or paper base.
Enlarger: a piece of darkroom equipment used for printing by the projection of light through the negative.
Exposure: the action of light on light-sensitive material to produce a picture. The duration of the exposure depends on the amount of light, aperture size, and exposure time.
Exposure meter: instrument to measure light levels and translate them into photographic exposure. Also called light meter and photo-electric exposure meter.
f/number (f/stop): number that indicates the amount of light a lens passes (taking into account its focal length), e.g., f/1.4, f/2, f/2.8, f/4, f/5.6, f/8, f/11, f/16, f/22, f/32, f/45, and f/64 (f/64 gives the least exposure). Each number passes half the amount of light of the preceding number.
Fast lens: one with large aperture (e.g., f/2), which enables pictures to be taken in poor lighting conditions.
Film speed: indicates how light-sensitive a film is. Fast films will record an image in low-level light conditions. Various systems exist for calibrating the speed of films but the best known are ASA and DIN ratings. Slow films give a finer and less "grainy" image.
Fixer: a solution that desensitizes emulsion by converting unexposed silver salts in the print/film to a soluble form so that they can be washed away.
Flare: bright patches on a picture caused by reflection inside the lens.
Flashbulbs/Flashcubes: expendable magnesium-filled bulbs that give a brilliant flash of light.
Flash synchronization: electric contact ensuring that a photographic flash fires at the moment the shutter is fully open.
Focal length: denotes the angle of view of a lens. Refers also to the distance from the center of the lens to the film, when the lens is focused at infinity.
Focal plane: the plane of sharpest focus (normally the film plane).
Fog: a veil of density over the

light-sensitive material caused by extraneous light or by chemical action.
Grain: the black metallic silver particles of which photographs (images) are made up and which can only be seen clearly with a microscope.
Graininess: apparent textured appearance of a print, negative, or transparency, caused by clumping of the grains making up the image. Grains are more pronounced with fast films, overdevelopment, and over-exposure.
Hypo: see fixer.
Infinity: one extreme end of the focusing scale on a camera. Generally a setting for subject about 100 or more feet away.
Latent image: the invisible image on film or paper after exposure and before development.
Lens hood: fits onto the front of lens barrel to prevent extraneous light from hitting the lens from outside the subject area. A lens hood helps prevent flare.
Monobath developer: processing solution which acts both as developer and fixer.
Multi-coating: thin films applied to separate elements of a lens to absorb extraneous light. Multi-coating absorbs more extraneous light than simple coating and therefore reduces flare more.
Neutral density filter: a colorless filter that cuts down the amount of light passing through it without changing the color of the light.
Normal lens: lens whose focal length approximately equals the diagonal of the camera negative.
Overexposure: an excessive amount of light reaching the light-sensitive material during exposure.
Parallax error: difference between the picture obtained by the taking lens and that shown by a viewing lens (or viewfinder), which is separated from it. Usually only significant in close-up work. Not present in SLR cameras.
Photoflood lamp: a high-intensity lamp used to give illumination.
Photo montage: combination of two or more photographic images by cut-and-paste techniques, multiple exposure in the camera, or combination printing.
Pinhole camera: simple camera in which the image is obtained by using a pinhole in an opaque material instead of a lens. A light-tight box with film or paper inside at one end and a pinhole at the other.
Positive: a print or transparency in which the tones and/or colors of the image correspond to those of the original subject.
Reciprocity failure: loss of film speed during long exposures – i.e., usually more than one second – or very short exposures – i.e., less than 1/1000th sec. Color film may also change its color balance slightly.
Safelight: a light with a filter (yellow, brown, red, green or orange) which can be used in a darkroom with light-sensitive papers and films.
Shutter: mechanism for allowing light to fall on the film for a controlled length of time. There are two basic types in modern cameras:
a) Focal plane (shutter) – this consists of two curtains that travel across the film, just in front of it. The slit between the curtains and the speed at which they travel can be varied to give exposure times ranging to 1/2000th sec.
b) Between the lens, or leaf (shutter) consists of a series of overlapping blades which are set in a circle within the lens. They open and close at speeds ranging from about 1 sec. to 1/500th sec.
SLR: single lens reflex (camera).
Spotting: filling in or bleaching tiny defects on a print.
Telephoto (or long focus) lens: one which includes less of the subject than a normal lens.
Transparency: a positive image suitable for projection.
"T": when on this setting the shutter opens when first pressed and closes when the shutter release is pressed a second time, thereby allowing an exposure of any amount of time.
Underexposure: an insufficient amount of light reaching the light-sensitive material during exposure.
Wetting agent: liquid which lowers the surface tension of water – helps avoid drying marks on film.
Wide angle (or short focus) lens: one which includes more of the subject than the normal lens.
Zoom lens: lens with a variable focal length and interlinked focus.

Index

Credits

Artists
Ilric Shetland

Photographs
Heather Angel: 5
Benson & Hedges Group: 21
Anne Bolt: 17 (bottom)
British Leyland: 20
Victor Burgin: 35 (right)
Centreprise: 88
Gerry Cranham: 26 (right)
Terry Dennett: 36
Derek Drage: 26 (left)
Jenny de Gex: 8
Glaxo Farley Foods Ltd: contents
Richard and Sally Greenhill: 11, 26 (middle), 29, 30, 44, 45, 50 (bottom), 53 (top), 54, 55, 56, 57, 60, 61, 62, 63, 64, 73, 74, 75
Hackney Flashers: 37
Paul Hill/Cooptic: 38
John Hillelson Agency: 11, 18, 19, 39, 85
John Hilliard: 79
Jamaica Tourist Board: 17 (top)
Kodak Museum: 15, 83
Margaret Murray: contents, 6, 7, 29 (left), 30, 31, 32, 49, 50 (top), 52, 53 (bottom), 59, 65, 67, 81
Margaret Murray/Christian Aid: 80
Parliament Hill Studios: 13
Popperfoto: contents, 10, 16, 84
Proctor & Gamble Italia: 22
Royal Photographic Society: 34
GeofSkinner: 9
Sotheby's Belgravia: 33
Jo Spence: 12, 14
Syndication International: 23
Topham/Chapman: contents
Topham/Sapieha: 35 (left)
Valerie Wilmer: 66, 78